DARWIN'S LUCK

Charles Darwin, not long after his return from the voyage of HMS *Beagle*. *Nora Barlow*, Charles Darwin's Diary of the Voyage of the Beagle, *Cambridge University Press, 1933* (The drawing has been attributed to George Raymond)

Darwin's Luck

Chance and Fortune in the Life and Work of Charles Darwin

Patrick H. Armstrong

continuum

Continuum UK, The Tower Building, 11 York Road, London SE1 7NX
Continuum US, 80 Maiden Lane, Suite 704, New York, NY 10038

www.continuumbooks.com

First published 2009

British Library Cataloguing-in-Publication Data
A catalogue record for this book is available from the British Library.

ISBN 978 184725 150 3

Typeset by Pindar NZ, Auckland, New Zealand
Printed and bound by MPG Books Ltd, Cornwall, Great Britain

Contents

Illustrations

For my children and grandchildren

Acknowledgements

As has been my custom with my previous writings on Darwin, I thank my late parents, Edward and Eunice Armstrong, for choosing to live in the university city of Cambridge at a formative stage of my life. Among my childhood recollections is often seeing Gwen Raverat, Charles Darwin's granddaughter, with an easel attached to her invalid chair, painting scenes along the Backs of the colleges, by the Mill Pond in Newnham, and on Laundress Green. Seeing her was one of the factors that generated in me a lifelong interest in the Darwin family. Later, I spent two periods of study-leave at Darwin College, Cambridge, the core of which is Newnham Grange, one-time home of Gwen and her family – a generation or two later than the days of Charles and Emma, Down House, and *On the Origin*. During one of these periods of leave I was introduced to the resources of the Darwin Collection by Peter Gautrey, former Curator of Manuscripts at the University Library.

I thank Bob Keenan of Pace University, New York, Paul Pearson of Cardiff University and Brian Shaw, of the University of Western Australia, who read chapters of the text: their friendship over the years has oft-times been an encouragement and a spur. A serendipitous meeting with Jim Moore, a distinguished Darwin scholar, in the Great Hall of my old college, University College, Durham gave me some important ideas. Michael Roberts I thank for interesting discussions on aspects of Charles Darwin's early life, and for hospitality in a delightful part of England.

A special thank you to my brother Tim and his wife Paula who have always most generously provided hospitality, just a stone's throw from Cambridge, always accompanied by what, in Australia, we call a larrikin sense of humour, whenever the Colonial drops out of the sky.

I thank Paul Pearson, John and Alison Underwood, and Gordon Chancellor for permission to use illustrations.

And Moyra, my dear wife Moyra, who has tolerated Charles Darwin and his nineteenth-century colleagues around the house in Nedlands for nearly 30 years ... Thank you, Darling.

St Deiniol's Library, Hawarden, North Wales has made me welcome many times, providing, as it does, an ideal environment for reading, thinking, writing and talking about almost any aspect of nineteenth-century thought.

This book was written during the tenure of an Adjunct Associate Professorship, at the Mount Lawley Campus of Edith Cowan University, Western Australia.

Nedlands, Western Australia
June 2008

Bibliographical Note

This is not the type of book in which the pages are loaded with footnotes: a few references have been given in the body of the text, but this note acknowledges some of the other published sources I have used or which may be of interest to readers.

Several important biographies have appeared in the last few decades. The first was Peter Brent (1981), *Charles Darwin: A Man Of Enlarged Curiosity* (Heinemann). John Bowlby was a distinguished psychiatrist, and wrote a 'psychological' account of Darwin's life and work in *Charles Darwin: a New Biography* in 1990 (Hutchinson). Adrian Desmond and James Moore's lively account simply entitled *Darwin* appeared a year later (Michael Joseph): it is extremely well researched – both authors are established Darwin scholars. Also massively authoritative is Janet Browne's two-volume work entitled *Charles Darwin: a Biography* (Jonathan Cape). The first volume, subtitled *Voyaging*, was published in 1995; the second – *The Power of Place* – appeared in 2002. All the above were published in London.

Emma Darwin's life has been treated by Edna Healey in *Emma Darwin: the Inspirational Wife of a Genius* (London: Headline, 2001). Darwin's teacher, friend and guide has attracted several biographers. From Lavenham in Suffolk, close to his parish of Hitcham, comes Jean Russell-Gebbett's *Henslow of Hitcham: Botanist, Educationalist and Clergyman* (Terence Dalton, 1977). More recently (2001), S. M. Walters and E. A. Stow published an attractive biography entitled *Darwin's Mentor: John Stevens Henslow, 1796–1861* (Cambridge University Press).

The *Beagle* voyage has an extensive literature: superbly illustrated, if now a little dated is Alan Moorehead's *Darwin and the 'Beagle'* (London: Hamish Hamilton, 1969). The distinguished Cambridge scientist, and great-grandson of Charles Darwin, Richard Keynes, published *Fossils, Finches and Fuegians* in 2002 (London: HarperCollins). Another member of the same family, Randal Keynes, looked at the life and death of Charles's daughter Annie in *Annie's Box: Charles Darwin, his Daughter and Human Evolution* (London: Fourth Estate, 2001). Charles's journal from the voyage was first published in 1933 (Cambridge University Press), edited by his granddaughter, Nora Barlow, with the title *Charles Darwin's Diary of the Voyage of HMS Beagle*. This is the most widely available edition and the one used here. There have been others.

Another granddaughter of Charles, Gwen Raverat, charmingly described growing up, in Cambridge and at Down, in the generation after the great naturalist's death – during the late Victorian and Edwardian period in *Period Piece: a Cambridge Childhood* (London: Faber and Faber, 1952; many subsequent editions). The book gives something of the feel of family life in the Darwin household.

Charles Darwin's *Autobiography* was first published in 1887, five years after his death. It was heavily edited by Darwin's family who, in an attempt to protect his reputation, deleted many passages they considered too personal or in some way controversial. A complete edition did not appear until 1959. An unedited paperback version was published in 1993 by W. W. Norton (New York) as *The Autobiography of Charles Darwin, 1809–1882*. It should be noted that it was written solely for the interest of his family, some 40 or more years after some of the events described, and sometimes the facts do not accord completely with other sources.

Cambridge University Press is progressively publishing *The Correspondence of Charles Darwin*. Volume 1 of this work of superb scholarship, including the letters written between 1821 and 1837, appeared in 1985. At the time of writing, the most recent volume was that dealing with the year 1867 (volume 15). The series has a distinguished editorial team, led by Frederick Burkhardt. Over five thousand of Darwin's letters have been placed online, along with many of his published works, his notes and ephemeral material: www.darwinproject.ac.uk provides a convenient entry point.

The topic of luck itself has been amusingly described by Richard Wiseman, in *The Luck Factor* (2004: Arrow, London; Hyperion, New York).

1

Introduction

Perhaps the most common view is that Charles Robert Darwin, the great Victorian naturalist, originator of the theory of evolution through natural selection, had something of a charmed life. He was born into a wealthy, upper-middle-class family, and never had to work for his living. He was extremely intelligent. He was educated at two of England's venerable educational institutions: Shrewsbury School, and Christ's College, Cambridge. At least while at Cambridge he had excellent teachers. He had the good fortune, at the very start of his scientific career, to be invited to accompany an important Royal Naval survey and exploration expedition, during which he had many of the resources of one of His Majesty's ships-of-war placed at his disposal. He married an attractive, intelligent heiress, who remained devoted to him. He was accorded high honours, being elected to a Fellowship of the Royal Society at a relatively young age (just before his thirtieth birthday), and held important and influential positions in the Geological Society of London and the British Association for the Advancement of Science. He was awarded an honorary degree by Cambridge, and other honours flowed from other universities and scientific bodies. He lived the better part of his life in a comfortable country house with a large garden, in relative seclusion, but conveniently close to the intellectual centre of London. His family was attended upon by a number of faithful servants. He had a network of supportive and very influential friends. He loved, and was loved by, his family, many of whom went on to distinguished careers themselves. In death he was given the highest honour his country could give: burial in Westminster

Abbey following a most impressive funeral in the presence of the great, the good and the powerful.

But there is another point of view. He had a somewhat demanding and at times rather difficult father. His mother died when he was only eight years of age, and in later life he said he could hardly remember her. He claimed that he 'learnt little' at Shrewsbury School. He then was sent to Medical School in Edinburgh, but hated the sight of operations being performed and left unqualified, to the chagrin of his doctor father. He required special tutoring to get him through some of his exams at Cambridge. He went on the exploration 'Voyage of the *Beagle*' but was seriously seasick much of the time. He was nearly shipwrecked and was ill several times in the course of the circumnavigation. His former girlfriend, of whom there is evidence he was at one stage extremely fond, married someone else when he was just a few months at sea. Of his ten children, three died before reaching adulthood. These included his dear, good, Annie and two others who died in early infancy, one of whom may have suffered from Down's syndrome. His brother Erasmus, to whom he was close, at least in youth, seems to have become affected by addiction to drugs. Charles Darwin was himself dogged by ill health throughout much of his life. His ideas and published works attracted much opprobrium in certain sections of society, and he was, following the publication of his most famous work, frequently attacked with quite ferocious outpourings of venom.

So, like most of us, he had times when fortune seemed to favour him, and moments when the fates seemed against him. He had a mix of good luck and ill luck: good times and bad times. And as with many of us, he made the best of opportunities that came his way. Occasionally circumstances that seemed unfortunate at the time had a 'silver lining'. Nevertheless, there were times in his life when he made a decision, or someone else took a decision, or circumstances occurred which profoundly influenced the direction of his life and work, and therefore had an effect on the development of his ideas, and thus on the thought-patterns of the modern world. This book attempts to identify some of those moments.

What is the nature of luck? Some people have the knack of being in the right place at the right time; of making advantageous business decisions and good decisions in their personal lives; of winning competitions and even lotteries. Success seems to follow success. Others seem accident-prone, seldom win at anything, and have lives strewn with mishaps that range from minor inconvenience to financial ruin.

Sometimes good luck or bad luck is indeed random, pernicious and due to 'pure chance'. Serendipity is everywhere! But recently scientific studies have been made of those who claim to be lucky or unlucky, particularly by Professor Richard Wiseman, a psychologist at the University of Hertfordshire in England. They seem to have shown that although there is a random element in the manner in which good fortune and ill fortune strike people there do seem to be certain psychological characteristics that those people who describe themselves as 'lucky' have in common. He summarized:

Lucky people tend to create, notice and act upon the chance opportunities in their lives.

Lucky people make successful decisions by using their intuition and 'gut feelings'.

Lucky people tend to be optimistic; their expectations concerning the future help them to fulfil their dreams and ambitions.

Lucky people are able to transform their bad luck into good fortune: to see the 'silver lining' behind every cloud. They tend to 'carry on regardless' and show determination in the face of ill fortune: in short to 'make their own luck'.

There is something vaguely Darwinian in this.

Darwin's work covered a great deal of science: he published in the fields of botany and zoology, geology and psychology, and he even ventured into what would now be considered anthropology. But his most notable contribution was the theory of evolution, or the transmutability of species as he sometimes preferred to call it, through natural selection. And an important component of natural selection is chance. Darwin's theory is based on the notion that organisms vary; some of those variations are random, or a matter of chance. The environment selects those individuals that are 'favoured' by characteristics that render them more able to survive and to pass their characteristics on to a new generation.

Charles Darwin seems to have been favoured by Providence. Abraham Lincoln, born the same day, also made his mark, but, perhaps, was less favoured. William Ewart Gladstone, four times British Prime Minister, was born in the same year and despite being unable to fulfil his greatest ambition – to bring peace to Ireland – would probably have said that fortune favoured him.

Charles Darwin's Origins

A basic component of Charles Darwin's concept of evolution, set out in *On the Origin of Species*, is the notion that the present is shaped by the past. Organisms that we can see around us today have a long antecedence: modern ideas on genetics have demonstrated how important is inheritance: what has gone before shapes the way things are now.

Yet we have no say in the selection of our parents. Like much in life it is a matter of chance, or luck, or Providence. Darwin was extremely fortunate in his genetic inheritance, together with his family background, and the financial security this provided.

Peter Brent, in his biography, reports of the yeoman Darwin family that 'Clever marriages and hard-headed management over several generations had brought the Darwins and their Lincolnshire estate of Marston prosperously into the seventeenth century'. But all this might have been lost, for in the Civil War William Darwin sided with the King, and as all the world knows, Charles I came to an unfortunate end during Cromwell's Commonwealth. However, on the Restoration he was compensated with a legal appointment: he became Recorder for Lincoln. His son married an Anne Waring, the daughter of a local landed family, introducing to the family a name that was to bounce down the generations, to the evolution Charles's great-uncle, to Charles's father, Robert Waring, and to the last of Charles's offspring, Charles Waring, who died in infancy. But Anne, an only daughter, also brought the Waring family estate, at Elston Hall in Nottinghamshire, whereat the Darwin family now established themselves. Several Darwins in these generations were interested in natural history, of which the most notable was Erasmus the polymath, the grandson of the first Darwin occupant of Elston Hall. Comfortably off small landowners they were, intelligent lawyers and medical men, with the preoccupations and interests of minor country squires. They had few links with the great landowning families or the aristocracy.

Robert Waring Darwin was the third son of Erasmus; like him he was elected a Fellow of the Royal Society, a dignity that along with some of the family names reappeared for several generations. Charles, three of his sons and a grandson were so honoured. There were, in the family down through the years, brilliant scientists, doctors, writers and artists, and there continue to be. Some might argue that a pattern of cousin marriages kept the money as well as the intellectual genes in the family. (The extent to which cousin marriages are damaging is even now disputed. Homozygosity – the result of breeding with a close relative – is normally considered to be bad, increasing the probability of acquiring certain inherited diseases. The possibility exists, however, that favourable characteristics might also be enhanced. Some recent genetic studies in Italy have suggested that cousin marriages increased the probability of very long life in the progeny. *New Scientist*, 26 January 2008.)

The Darwin family tale that, when Dr Darwin, Charles Darwin's father, arrived in Shrewsbury in 1787, having trained in medicine in Edinburgh and at Leiden in Holland, he had £20 to his name, was probably apocryphal, but is indicative of the respect that the family accorded him for his ability to make money. Besides his medical degrees, and his genetic inheritance from his distinguished father Erasmus Darwin – doctor, poet, essayist, polymath – he had modest inheritances from his mother and his aunt. He commenced by investing in houses in Shrewsbury, and then as the rents and the income from the medical practice began to accrue, he started to invest in the important capitalist ventures of the Industrial Revolution that was accelerating close by. Biographer Janet Browne has listed Robert Darwin's investments and financial affairs in some detail. He was an important shareholder in the Trent and Mersey Canal. Thomas Telford, one of the great engineers of the age, who lived close by in Shrewsbury for a time, may have been a contact he used for some of his investments, for the doctor invested in Telford's Holyhead

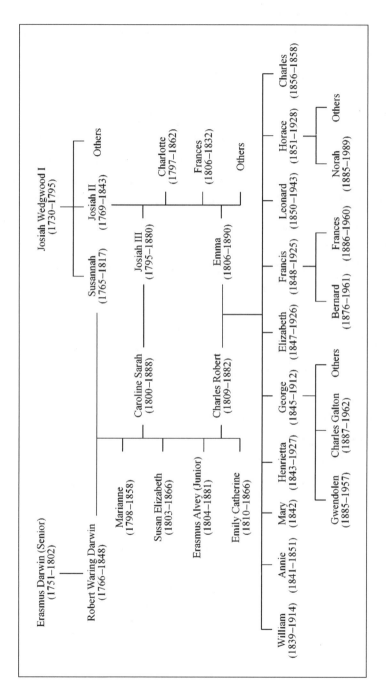

1. Family tree of the Darwin and Wedgwood families

Road, which linked England's industrial districts to the port of Holyhead in Anglesey and thence to Ireland. He invested also in the Ellesmere Canal that linked the various navigable rivers of north-west England.

In the days before the joint stock banks emerged as important money brokers and grantors of mortgages, well-to-do professional men such as Robert Waring Darwin filled this role. Although decidedly Whig in politics, and privately contemptuous of the inherited privileges of the aristocracy and landed gentry, he was not averse to taking their money in medical fees and in lending them money on mortgages over their property. In 1837 he lent Lord Berwick £10,200, and gave Viscount Clive a mortgage of £15,000. The father of Charles's erstwhile girlfriend, Squire Owen of Woodhead, also owed him a substantial sum, as did Sir John Hammer, Member of Parliament for Shrewsbury. Smaller farmers and businessmen in the district might borrow a couple of thousand or a few hundred. There were also small rural and farm landholdings that produced modest rents, and there was a bedrock of safe government bonds: he had over £20,000 in 3 per cent and 4 per cent Consols.

His link with the Wedgwood pottery family, through his wife Susannah, also contributed to his prosperity. She owned one fifth of the Etruria pottery works in Staffordshire. On the death of her father, Josiah Wedgwood I, the founder of the dynasty, in 1795, she inherited £25,000.

Dr Darwin's income from medical fees varied from around £1,822 in the early years of his practice, to £3,000. The average was between £2,000 and £2,500. This probably represented about a third of his total income. It is claimed that his estate, on his death in 1848, was worth £223,759. (His father Erasmus left £35,930; his son Charles was worth £146,911 7s. 10d. at death.) Bearing in mind the change in the value of money, this would put Dr Robert Darwin close to the level of the billionaires of the early twenty-first century! The word scrupulous has sometimes been used for Dr Darwin, and certainly his keeping of accounts – what came in and what was dispersed – was often meticulous. Bearing in mind his wealth, the establishment at The Mount, the home he built overlooking the River Severn, seems to have been fairly frugal. But he made careful provision for all his children (both sons and daughters) and his elderly servants. When his tenants had difficulties in paying rent he occasionally waived it or allowed a debtor to postpone payment. Nevertheless he did not like to have someone get the better of him, and he took legal action, even against folk related to him, in attempts to secure what he felt he was owed, not always successfully, although he had an astute lawyer, a certain Thomas Salt, solicitor.

Charles came to realize in early manhood that his father was likely to leave him with sufficient property for him never to have to work if he did not wish to do so. Good fortune indeed. Nevertheless, in his own home later in life the habits of a modest frugality, or 'elegant economy' as novelist Mrs Gaskell put it, inculcated at The Mount, seem to have continued. He had been brought up accustomed to modest comfort, but not to reckless extravagance.

Let us now look at the personality and character of Charles's father, Dr Robert Waring Darwin (1766–1848) in a little more detail. He must have had an imposing presence. He was tall, and very portly. He at one stage weighed 24 stone (about 152kg). He had a part-circle cut out of the dining room table to accommodate his large belly. He had a man go ahead of him when, on his doctor's rounds, he was called to a house he had not visited before, to check whether the floors would stand his weight. He does not seem to have been tyrannical, but to have imposed his presence on a gathering, or a conversation, whenever he came into a room. Charles was to write of him that he was 'the kindest man I ever met': but they had their differences and Dr Robert does not seem to have suffered fools gladly. The failure of Charles to make good progress at Shrewsbury School, his dropping out of the medical course at Edinburgh, his son's preoccupation with shooting and collecting beetles, and initially at least, the suggestion that he join the *Beagle* voyage must have tried him sorely. They certainly at times had an uneasy relationship. Charles sometimes expressed the view that his father did not particularly like him. Emma, in later life, thought that this was unfair.

3

To Lose One Parent is a Misfortune: Childhood and Adolescence

Charles's mother Susannah died of an abdominal tumour in July 1817 when she was only 52, and he was just 8 years old. He said in his *Autobiography* that he could 'hardly remember anything about her, except her deathbed, her black velvet gown and her curiously constructed work table'. In another account, written earlier, he said that he had a vague recollection of one or two walks with her, but that he had 'no distinct remembrance of any conversation'. This was, he thought, partly because of his sisters, 'owing to their great grief never being able to speak about her or mention her name'. This does not seem to be simply lack of familiarity, because there are few mentions in family correspondence (which is full of references to the childhood illnesses of the family) of her becoming ill until a few months before her death. It does seem, however, that the children were kept from seeing her in the final few weeks, when her sister Kitty reported that 'her suffering is terrible'. Yet Charles also recalls his father crying the day she died (it must have been harrowing for the pre-eminent doctor in Shrewsbury not to be able to do much for his dying wife, lying racked with pain). Apart from that, nothing. No warm recollections, no loving remembrances. As one biographer has put it: 'We know the wound was there, because the scar remained. A healed-over scar perhaps, but a scar nevertheless.' John Bowlby, a consultant psychiatrist who wrote a 'psychological' biography of Darwin, stated that 'there can be little doubt that Charles was correct in attributing his lack of memory to the wall of silence built by his elder sisters'. He goes on to suggest that this wall of silence had an effect on his emotional development.

The gap was to a considerable extent filled by his covey of sisters. The eldest was Marianne, nearly 11 years older than Charles, who seems to have taken a leading part in nursing her mother in her final weeks, and appears to have thereafter fallen into the role of household manager. But within seven years of her mother's death she was married. So then Susan and Caroline took over the matriarchal role. It was Susan to whom he usually wrote from the *Beagle* a few years later as his 'Dear Old Granny', a salutation that suggests both a note of respect and a special affection. Caroline seems to have had a dominating personality, but nevertheless this was accompanied by a strong sense of humour. Charles later variously described her as a 'mother to me in the early part of my life' and 'my Governess'. Her cousin, Frank Wedgwood, remarked that 'she looked like a duchess'; it was she who wrote to Charles in 1826: 'I must say, dear Charles how happy I am that you have been studying the bible.' Rather earlier it was Susan who expressed pleasure at his being 'such a good boy with your French'. And it was Susan who perhaps had the strongest social conscience: she is reported as being 'hot about slavery'; but she was also concerned for her brothers' welfare, insisting that they wore flannel in the cold weather. And then there was little Catherine, a year younger than Charles, and who seems to have been his special friend. They seem to have played much together: he told his own sons that he had a special affinity with her; they had their own green hiding place in a sweet chestnut tree. Yet she, too, was not on occasion averse to correcting his spelling or imparting some other sisterly piece of advice. The two youngest were taught the rudiments, in their early years by Caroline, who Charles later described as 'kind, clever and zealous'.

The 'sisterhood' seem to have doted on the youngest male of the family: they encouraged him, cared for him and periodically chided him, Caroline particularly. Their love surged over him, perhaps giving something that his mother, sickly, and old before her time, might not have been able to provide had she lived.

And what about elder brother Erasmus, some four years his senior? Charles Darwin wrote in his *Autobiography* that their 'minds and tastes were … so different' that he did not think that he owed him much intellectually.

But when young they shared an interest in science and there are a number of grounds for believing that in several very real ways 'Eras' or 'Ras' went ahead and prepared the way for the younger boy. It seems that Erasmus may have intervened on his behalf occasionally in the rough and tumble of the rather brutal regime of Shrewsbury School (of which more anon). There was an incident in which a complaint was made by Erasmus, possibly on behalf of his young brother, about a damp mattress! The elder lad encouraged Charles to read, and lent him books. They turned the garden shed at The Mount, the family home overlooking the River Severn at Shrewsbury, into a laboratory. They did experiments there (Dr Darwin would not allow such activities in the house), and Charles's nickname at the time was 'Gas'! Even after Erasmus left for Cambridge in 1822 he attempted to provide a measure of supervision. One letter read:

> I am very glad to hear that all glass & earthenware apparatus has arrived safe ... I should recommend ye first two or three shillings there to spare in ye Lab, to have a shelf put up in ye place over ye retort shelf ... The 10L which poor Miss Congreve has left ... will come in very nicely for an Air Pump ... As far as I can make out you are not carrying on any experiments in ye Lab. I will recommend you a few which will employ you some time, & will not be expensive.

These included extracting the silver from a sixpence, and obtaining pure alumina from alum. Some of these suggestions came from witnessing experiments done by Professor John Henslow, then the Professor of Mineralogy at Cambridge, and later the Professor of Botany. The demonstrations were described by Erasmus as 'very entertaining'. Ras added that the series of lectures he had attended had been Henslow's 'first course ... he will have improved by the time you come up'. It was taken for granted that Charles would follow his elder brother to Cambridge. Erasmus had also made contact with another person with whom Charles would have important dealings: in 1822–3 he wrote to Charles to say he might shortly obtain some rock specimens that had been described to him by Professor Adam Sedgwick, who held the Chair of Geology, from the Gog Magog Hills – low chalk undulations just a few miles outside Cambridge. Yet another way in which

Erasmus helped to prepare Charles – from the age of about eleven – for later challenges was through taking him on long horseback excursions into North Wales – sometimes as long as 30 miles a day across the mountains, developing horsemanship skills that were to prove valuable in South America.

And it continued; while Charles was on the *Beagle*, his brother Ras sought out books for him and arranged for them to be forwarded to distant parts of the world. He helped by receiving some of the specimens he sent home. After his return, by then already established in literary London, and knowing the ways of the capital, Erasmus provided accommodation for his younger brother at 34 Great Marlborough Street, as he began the tasks of sorting and classifying his specimens, and writing up his material. At Shrewsbury, at Christ's College, Cambridge, and later in London Erasmus had 'gone before' or had looked out for his younger brother. Charles was fortunate that it was so.

But we must first double back a little. Susannah Darwin (née Wedgwood) was a Unitarian – the most liberal of the Nonconformist denominations – and she took her children with her to the Unitarian chapel in Shrewsbury. Charles was briefly sent to a small school run by a Mr Case, the Unitarian minister. However, it seems that, unsurprisingly, the Unitarian influence declined with Susannah's passing. It was probably not thought that the family of the town's leading medical doctor (a closet agnostic) should be too conspicuous, and to balance things somewhat, Charles had been baptized in St Chad's Anglican church, nearby. A little later he was sent to Shrewsbury School, a public school headmastered by an Anglican clergyman of the most traditional outlook, Dr Samuel Butler. Charles claimed that he learnt little there: Latin and Greek dominated the curriculum, and rote-learning was the pedagogic method commonly employed. Too strident a proclamation of Unitarian dissent might have been an impediment when he was sent to Christ's College, Cambridge with a view to his becoming a Church of England clergyman (like his cousin, William Darwin Fox). But the Anglican thread in his background and education enabled him to move easily into Cambridge, where many of the professors and teachers were in Holy Orders of the Church of England.

But Cambridge for Charles came a little later. Not long after Charles's sixteenth birthday, Dr Darwin felt that his younger son was not making the progress that he ought at Shrewsbury School. Perhaps too much time was being spent in that tool-shed laboratory, or wandering in the Shropshire countryside, sometimes aimlessly, sometimes collecting natural history specimens (particularly beetles), or in shooting and fishing. Charles admitted that he was learning little. He later recalled: 'Nothing could have been worse for the development of my mind than Dr Butler's school ... The school as a means of education to me was simply a blank.' In the early summer of 1825, therefore, he recalled in his *Autobiography*:

> As I was doing no good at school, my father wisely took me away at a rather earlier age than usual, and sent me (October, 1825) to Edinburgh University with my brother ... [who] was completing his medical studies, though I do not believe he ever really intended to practise, and I was sent to commence them.

Dr Darwin obviously felt that the lad needed some direction, a clear focus, and some solid hard work. Charles was taken by his father on his medical rounds, mixing medicines and assisting with some minor medical chores. He wrote:

> At one time I had at least a dozen patients, and I felt a keen interest in the work. My father, who was by far the best judge of character I ever knew, declared that I should make a good successful physician, meaning ... one who got many patients.

The stage was set for the young Darwin to follow his father and grandfather into a prosperous medical career. But it didn't work out like that.

Charles and Erasmus left for Edinburgh together in October 1825. There is evidence that here, again, Ras took the initiative in some ways. He seems to have been the instigator of, for example, expanding their reading by getting books out of the library or some of their explorations in and around the city, and was possibly something of a guiding hand in Charles's medical studies (Erasmus had virtually completed his).

But in spite of his elder brother's guidance things were going wrong. A Dr Duncan lectured on *Materia Medica*. Charles wrote to motherly Caroline about 'a long stupid lecture' from him. 'Dr Duncan is so very learned that his wisdom has left no room for sense,' he complained. Dr Munro on Anatomy and Pathology seems to have been worse: 'I dislike him & his lectures so much I cannot speak with decency about them. He is so dirty in person & actions.' The young Darwin also enrolled in some geology lectures, although they were not essential for his course, given by Professor Robert Jameson. He found them 'incredibly dull'. Jameson taught that many rocks, even igneous rocks, were formed by precipitation from a primeval ocean, an idea that was already falling into disrepute.

Letters from 'Granny' Susan passed on Dr Darwin's concern at the manner in which Charles seemed to be picking and choosing which lectures he attended, and particularly at the thought he had expressed that he might be 'coming home before the course of lectures were finished'. He was fervently encouraged not to do so.

But worst of all were the operations, performed, of course, without anaesthetics. He watched two that were 'very bad … one on a child, but rushed away before they were completed'. These two cases 'fairly haunted' him 'for many a long year'.

On the face of it, the two Edinburgh years were a failure. He found that he hated medicine … and he found that he had no interest in it. If his letters and the recollections he recorded in his *Autobiography* over 40 years later are anything to go by, most of the lectures were excruciatingly dull. He left unqualified. Dr Darwin was not best pleased. A terrible misfortune? A waste of time?

As during the days at Shrewsbury School, so in Edinburgh it was from his extracurricular activities that he gained the most benefit. He took books out of the university library on many aspects of zoology – particularly entomology and conchology (the study of shelled creatures). He went for walks along the Firth of Forth seeking out sea creatures. Three days before his seventeenth birthday, on 9 February 1826, he made the following annotation:

Caught a sea mouse, Aphrodita Aculeata, of Linneaus … when its mouth was touched it tried to coil itself in a ball, but was very inert; Turton states that it has only two feelers, does not Linneaus say 4? I thought I perceived them.

Detailed observation, careful comparison of his own observations with those of others, and an emphasis on both the behaviour of an organism and its appearance. Not bad for a 16 year old!

There were other advantages too. He learnt to preserve and stuff birds, paying his teacher of taxidermy a guinea an hour. His instructor was the black former servant of Dr Duncan, who had once worked with the explorer Charles Waterman, author of *Wanderings in South America*. Maybe working with this man inoculated him against racial prejudice: on his voyage he was able to get along with men and women of many races.

Despite his scathing references to Robert Jameson, he went on geological field trips with him into the nearby hills, and attended practical classes on the identification of rocks. He made friends with some of the fishermen at nearby Newhaven, occasionally accompanying them when they trawled for oysters, obtaining some interesting specimens. He studied them carefully, and following his election to the Plinian Society on 28 November 1826 he gave talks on what he had found. The Plinian Society had been founded in 1823, and was made up of both established scientists and young students. It was a forum for unorthodox views, and the university's professors seldom attended. Darwin was proposed for membership by a young, anti-clerical firebrand, Willam Browne: a week later he was on the society's council. Not long after the 18 year old joined the society, a young student contemporary, William Greg, gave a paper in which he advocated the idea that the 'lower animals possess every faculty and propensity of the human mind'. Later, firebrand Browne suggested that the human mind, and indeed consciousness, had an entirely material basis. These ideas flew hard in the face of religious orthodoxy, and vigorous discussion followed; indeed the reports on the talk and the preceding announcement of the talk were expunged from the society's records. The young naturalist's eyes were being opened to the nature of scientific controversy; he learned how to prepare (admittedly short) scientific papers and to deliver them. And Charles also came to appreciate the important idea that the behaviour of creatures was as interesting as their appearance.

But perhaps the most important contact that Darwin made at the

Plinian Society was Dr Robert Grant, soon to be appointed to the Chair of Comparative Anatomy and Zoology at the infant London University. He befriended Charles, and took him as a guest to meetings of the Wernian Society, a much more senior and distinguished organization than the radical Plinian. Grant was 16 years older than Darwin, medically qualified, but already establishing a name for himself as a zoologist. They went on excursions along the Firth of Forth coast, and together dissected some of the creatures they found there; they cooperated on studies of sea-mats (*Flustra*) and the parasites found inside oyster shells. Straightforward enough, perhaps, were it not that Grant was profoundly influenced by French zoological thought, particularly that of evolutionist Jean-Baptiste Lamarck, and saw some of these primitive creatures as being close to the root of the animal kingdom. Darwin was exposed to the mind of yet another naturalist who was prepared to challenge existing orthodoxies.

Finally, the little medicine that Darwin learned *did* later prove of some value to him, for example in describing the physiognomy of indigenous peoples he met on the *Beagle* voyage. Here are his notes from his diary entry for 22 December 1835, on tattooing by the Maori people in New Zealand:

> The complicated but symmetrical figures, covering the whole face, puzzle & mislead the unaccustomed eye; it is moreover probable that the deep incisions, by destroying the play of the superficial muscles, would give an air of rigid inflexibility.

In looking through his notes on the effects of stinging creatures on bringing up 'pustules' on his skin, or the effects of opium addiction on some of the Indian indentured workers in Mauritius, one can sometimes hear the faint echo of the days at Edinburgh Medical School, together with that summer's brief apprenticeship with Dr Darwin and the voice of the *medicin manqué*. And this training also may have contributed to his interest in, and curiosity about, people of all races.

'To lose one parent ... may be regarded as a misfortune', Lady Bracknell declaimed in *The Importance of Being Earnest*, but somehow Charles seems to have covered over this loss in his mind. And the void left by his mother was filled by his doting sisterhood and his elder brother – the latter 'going before him' in a number of ways, and preparing the ground. The influence of these siblings was certainly benign, and might have been less intense, and certainly would have been different, had his mother lived. The disappearance of his mother may just possibly have reduced the Unitarian influence which might have been a disadvantage academically and socially. His time at Shrewsbury School he regarded as little less than an academic disaster: although his marks were not all that bad, he learnt very little there that was of future use to him. But his poor performance there resulted in his removal and his introduction to medical work with his father, followed by the two academic years in Edinburgh. These were wasted years as far as his official, paternally approved medical studies were concerned, but in what he read, the societies and meetings he attended, the people he met, the introduction he received to the techniques of natural history observation and recording, in seeing how established ideas could be questioned, and in generally learning how science functioned, the training for what followed could hardly have been bettered. Out of a series of disasters came sound preparation. It has been suggested that in Edinburgh, initially under the watchful eye of his brother, Charles Darwin 'learnt how to learn', acquiring skills he was able to put into effect in Cambridge later. He learnt the importance of reading widely (outside his field of study), of the possibility of questioning established opinion, of field studies and collecting natural history specimens, and of making the personal acquaintance of scientific men. He was learning from his mistakes, and learning to make the best of opportunities that came his way.

But Dr Darwin cared little for much of this. The family medical tradition and the long link with Edinburgh Medical School had been interrupted. 'You care for nothing but shooting, dogs and ratcatching', he exploded at one stage in his son's youth. 'You will be a disgrace to yourself and all your family.' As far as Robert Waring Darwin was concerned, it looked as though his younger son's luck had run out. To prevent his turning into 'an idle sporting man', some other form of pressure would have to be applied. Dr Darwin, notwithstanding his own scepticism in matters of religion, as has already been hinted, sent him to Cambridge to prepare for the Church of England priesthood.

4

Cambridge: It's Who You Know as Much as What You Know

Darwin, in his *Autobiography*, looking back after many years, stated that he thought that his time at Cambridge was 'sadly wasted there and worse than wasted'. The picture of the 'idle sporting man' so much feared by his father comes through:

> From my passion for shooting and for hunting and when this failed, for riding across country I got into the sporting set, including some dissipated low-minded young men. We often used to dine together in the evening, though these dinners often included men of a higher stamp, we sometimes drank too much, with jolly singing and playing cards afterwards.

To be fair, when editing these reminiscences for publication years later, his son Francis Darwin enquired about these revelries from some of Charles's contemporaries, and gathered he had 'exaggerated the Bacchanalian nature of some of these parties'.

The habit of picking and choosing which lectures he would attend, established in Edinburgh, persisted: he was 'so sickened' by the Edinburgh lectures that he did not attend some courses that he realized later would have been of value to him. He attempted mathematics but, he recalled: 'I got on very slowly. The work was repugnant to me.' He went on: 'With respect to Classics I did nothing except attend a few compulsory college lectures, and the attendance was purely nominal.' Study of Euclid, however, he enjoyed. Perhaps in this enjoyment of geometrical reasoning we can see the progenitor of his ability to see in three dimensions, so much an advantage, as he put it himself later, 'in making out the geology of a country'. Euclidian geometry also involves logical argument and deduction; in later life Darwin excelled in these.

He admitted, however, that he was one of the candidates who, ever to the annoyance of the academic staff of universities, was able to 'work with some earnestness' for 'a month or two' before an examination and gain a satisfactory, if not outstanding, pass.

He struggled to get back the Latin and Greek that had been drummed into him when he was such a reluctant pupil at Shrewsbury School. He had to read William Paley's *Evidences for Christianity* and *Moral Philosophy*, the logic of which he admired. He also studied Paley's *Natural Theology*; not on the syllabus, but widely read by his contemporaries. He remarks in his *Autobiography*, somewhat backhandedly:

> The careful study of these works, without attempting to learn any part by rote, was the only part of the Academical Course which, as I then felt and as I still believe, was of the least use to me in the education of my mind. I did not at that time trouble myself about Paley's premises; and taking these on trust I was charmed and convinced by the long line of argumentation.

This is profoundly significant. *On the Origin of Species* owes a great deal to Paley's *Natural Theology*. There are indeed those who have remarked that *On the Origin* is the last work of natural theology, as much as the first of modern evolutionary biology. (Natural theology argued that the extraordinary complexity, beauty and coherence of the natural world provided evidence for the existence of a Creator, and by studying plants and animals, and the way in which they were exquisitely adapted to their environment and way of life, one could gain insights into the mind of the Creating God.) It is partly surmise, but what Darwin seems to have gained from Paley's works is his appreciation of organisms' adaptations to their environment and way of life, and his logical, step by step method of developing his ideas. A single quotation from Paley's book illustrates the approach:

> The air-bladder also of a *fish* affords a plain and direct instance, not only of contrivance ... The principle of the contrivance is clear; the application of the

principle is also clear. The use of the organ to sustain, and, ... to elevate, the body of the fish in the water, is proved by observing, what has been tried, that, when the bladder is burst, the fish grovels at the bottom ... The manner in which the purpose is attained, and the suitableness of the means to the end, are not difficult to be apprehended. The rising and sinking of a fish in water, so far as it is independent of the stroke of the fins and tail, can only be regulated by the specific gravity of the body. When the bladder, contained in the body of the fish, is contracted ..., the bulk of the fish is contracted along with it; whereby, since the absolute weight remains the same, the specific gravity, which is the sinking force, is increased, and the fish descends: on the contrary, when, in consequence of the relaxation of the muscles, the elasticity of the inclosed and now compressed air, restores the dimensions of the bladder, the tendency downwards becomes proportionably less than it was before, or is turned into a contrary tendency. (William Paley, *Natural Theology*, 1807 edition, pages 243–5.)

On the Origin can be seen as 'one long argument'. Facts are presented, and the consequences of those facts considered, possible objections are raised, and then answered, gradually building to a conclusion. Indeed it could be said that the entire corpus of Darwin's work presents 'one long argument', for *Variation of Animals and Plants Under Domestication, Descent of Man, Expression of Emotions in Man and Animals* and some of his later botanical works are all in fact developments of Darwin's evolutionary hypothesis. They all owe much to his reading of Paley.

Another important influence was the Reverend Professor John Stevens Henslow, Professor of Botany. Although he was the author of over 130 publications, including a number of books, on topics as varied as agriculture, archaeology, botany, geology, zoology and theology, he was an educational pioneer (developing the teaching of natural history in schools and enthusiastically promoting museums), was a political pamphleteer and held the Cambridge Chairs, first of Mineralogy, and later of Botany, John Henslow (1796–1861) will for ever primarily be remembered as Darwin's teacher, and the person influential in gaining for him his position on the *Beagle*.

In many ways Henslow was a typical example of that supremely important figure in British science, the Victorian clergyman-naturalist. He came from a reasonably well-to-do, upper-middle-class family. His father (John Prentis

2. John Stevens Henslow by T. H. Maguire, Darwin's teacher at Cambridge, and lifelong
friend. *National Portrait Gallery*

Henslow) was a solicitor, but later went into business with his uncle as a wine merchant in Rochester, Kent. John Stevens was born on 6 February 1796, the eldest of eleven children, three of whom died in infancy. Both his parents collected natural history specimens, and their bright young son took after them. Boarding school on the outskirts of London followed; here his interest in natural history was further encouraged. And then, on to St John's College, Cambridge, a large and wealthy college. He studied mathematics and philosophy, but also attended lectures in chemistry, geology and mineralogy. He graduated 16th Wrangler (sixteenth on the class-list of those who obtained first class honours in mathematics) in 1818, having won several university prizes. He remained in Cambridge after graduating helping professors with their researches, and in preparing demonstrations for students. He undertook several geological expeditions to different parts of the British Isles – the Isle of Wight and the Isle of Man in 1819, and the Isle of Anglesey in 1820 and 1821. He was elected to the Chair of Mineralogy in May 1822 (at what would these days be considered the extremely young age of 26), commencing his lecturing in early 1823.

Typically, he married Harriet Jenyns, the daughter of a country clergyman from a landowning family in December 1823 (in those times, English landed and clerical families were frequently connected by kinship and marriage). This link too was important to Darwin, because it was to Leonard Jenyns, Harriet's brother, that Charles Darwin turned when he required someone to catalogue, study and describe the fish specimens that he brought back from the voyage of the *Beagle*.

John Stevens Henslow was ordained deacon in April 1824, and priest in November of the same year, immediately prior to his taking the position of 'perpetual curate' (more or less the equivalent to vicar) of Little St Mary's Church, Cambridge. The following year he added to his list of appointments (and presumably his income) by accepting the Chair of Botany. The holding of more than one church and university appointment at the same time was not considered particularly unusual. However, within a year or two he had given up the Mineralogy Chair in order to concentrate on the Botany professorship.

Professor Henslow was an excellent teacher, delivering well-prepared lectures, illustrated by diagrams of his own construction. Of even greater importance was his agreeable, affable manner: he was at ease with the most distinguished scholar yet also the youngest student (or schoolchild), and answered queries, no matter how naïve, with care and with courtesy, acknowledging that whatever observation was brought to him was a matter of interest and importance.

It was around this time that Henslow commenced holding his Friday evening soirées, for anyone in Cambridge who was interested in science. These became something of an institution, and some very distinguished personages attended, including, in March 1828, the American artist-ornithologist, John James Audubon (1785–1851).

In 1829 Charles Darwin attended some of Henslow's soirées, as well as some of his lectures, and their lifelong friendship was established. They went for botanical excursions into the Cambridgeshire countryside and Darwin became known as 'the man who walks with Henslow'. In May 1830 Charles wrote to his cousin, W. D. Fox:

> I have seen a good deal of Henslow lately, & the more I see of him the more I like him.

The tuition that Charles Darwin obtained in these various informal and formal ways was of great significance in the young naturalist's development: Darwin himself acknowledged that his meeting with Professor Henslow was the one event 'which influenced my career more than any other'.

In the spring and early summer of 1831 Henslow encouraged Darwin to take an interest in geology, and a few weeks later suggested his name as a possible companion for Captain Robert FitzRoy on the *Beagle* voyage (see Chapter 5). Henslow also directed Darwin's reading constructively, suggesting, for example, that he take with him Charles Lyell's *Principles of Geology* on the voyage, although he cautioned his young friend that 'on no account' should he accept all that was in it! Also, in the frantic period of planning for departure, Henslow gave important advice on the preparation, preservation, storage and transport of specimens.

While Darwin was away on the *Beagle*, the two kept in contact by letter.

Consignments of specimens were sent to Henslow for preliminary sorting and safe-keeping – the first box was received in 1833 – and extracts from Darwin's letters were printed and circulated. Thus when Darwin returned from the sea the scientific communities of Cambridge and London already knew something about him. Henslow later studied some of the plant specimens Darwin had collected on the voyage, writing papers on the flora of the Galapagos and the Cocos Islands on the basis of Darwin's collected material.

In 1839 Henslow gave up his Cambridge house, and most of his Cambridge commitments, moving to the parish of All Saints, Hitcham, a small village in Suffolk, about 35 miles (56 km) from Cambridge. He retained his university professorship, but concentrated his teaching into a few weeks of the year. He was rector of this small rural parish for the rest of his life. The link with Charles Darwin continued, through correspondence, to the benefit of both parties, although Henslow, a liberal churchman in some ways, never entirely accepted the conclusions expressed in *On the Origin of Species*.

Henslow's final illness seems to have had its onset in mid-March 1861, when he caught a severe cold on a visit to friends in the south of England. He returned to Hitcham on 23 March, with chest pains and having difficulty in breathing. Doctors were summoned, but little could be done for him in a world without antibiotics. He lingered for some weeks, with several of his former colleagues and family members around him. He was described in those days as being 'calm, resigned and quite happy … full of peace and love'. He died on 16 May 1861, at the relatively young age of 65, and was buried next to his wife, who pre-deceased him by a few years, just a few feet from the church tower in the wildflower-filled Hitcham churchyard. His gravestone is surrounded by ox-eye daisies, buttercups and knapweed, and is covered with lichens. Swallows nest nearby in the church porch.

Darwin continued to be influenced by his friend and erstwhile teacher long after Henslow had died. He constructed a heated glasshouse at his home at Downe in Kent in 1863, and it was in the years following this that he did some of his best botanical experimental work. His correspondence – for example with botanist Joseph Hooker – shows that he was frequently using

Henslow's writings, particularly his *Principles of Descriptive and Physiological Botany* (1835).

Charles Darwin's assessment of the Rev Professor Henslow, given in the *Autobiography* he wrote for his family late in life (1873), read as follows:

> His strongest taste was to draw conclusions from long-continued minute observations. His judgement was excellent and his whole mind well balanced, but I do not suppose that anyone would say that he possessed much original genius.

To which biographers S. M. Walters and E. A. Stow add (in *Darwin's Mentor: John Stevens Henslow 1796–1861*, published in 2001):

> [F]or the progress of science as for the welfare of mankind, a flair for teaching which releases genius may be as important as the genius itself. Without Henslows there are no Darwins.

The second important clergyman professor that Darwin met at Cambridge was Professor Adam Sedgwick. There were, until the first half of the twentieth century, families in which for many generations all the sons became clergymen of the Church of England, and all the daughters married into parsonages. As we have already seen, clerical families thus comprised a tight network, held together by the bonds of kinship and marriage. This network, in the Victorian period, was one of the sustaining structures of English intellectual (particularly scientific) life. Adam Sedgwick was in many ways a typical product of this network. He was himself the son of a country clergyman, the Vicar of Dent, in Yorkshire. He was born in March 1785, and when young he wandered through the Yorkshire countryside, collecting natural history specimens. He attended school in the nearby town of Sedbergh, and then went on to Trinity College, Cambridge. He became a Fellow of his College in 1810, and was ordained in 1817. He was, to the surprise of some, including perhaps himself, appointed Woodwardian Professor of Geology in 1818. He had no special knowledge of geology, and he is said to have declaimed at the time: 'Hitherto I have never turned a stone; henceforth I shall leave no stone unturned.' His prediction was borne out. He was to become a giant of what has been called the 'Heroic Age' of geology, the period when the main geological time-periods were defined, and the fundamental concepts underlying the subject established. Sedgwick was responsible for describing the Cambrian system (from Cambria, the Latin name for Wales, where much of the fieldwork was done), the series of rocks containing fossils of some of the oldest and most primitive forms of life.

While these researches were continuing, Sedgwick and the young Charles Darwin became friendly; Henslow, as we have seen, encouraged this friendship, and in the early summer of 1831, Professor Sedgwick spent the night at the Darwin family home in Shrewsbury before taking Darwin on a geological field trip through North Wales, providing him with an excellent grounding in field geology. Darwin later described the trip as follows:

> As I had come up to Cambridge at Christmas, I was forced to keep two terms after passing my final examination, at the commencement of 1831; and Henslow then persuaded me to begin the study of geology. Therefore on my return to Shropshire I examined sections and coloured a map of parts round Shrewsbury. Professor Sedgwick in the beginning of August intended to visit North Wales to pursue his famous geological investigation amongst the older rocks, and Henslow asked him to allow me to accompany him. Accordingly he came and slept in my Father's house ...
>
> Next morning we started for Llangollen, Conway, Bangor and Capel Curig. This tour was of decided use in teaching me a little how to make out the geology of a country. Sedgwick often sent me on a line parallel to his, telling me to bring back specimens of the rocks and to mark the stratification on a map. I have little doubt that he did this for my own good, as I was too ignorant to have aided him ... At Capel Curig I left Sedgwick and went in a straight line by compass and map across the mountains to Barmouth, never following any track unless it coincided with my course. I thus came on some strange wild places and enjoyed much this manner of travelling. (*Autobiography*)

Darwin used, in his explorations during the *Beagle* voyage, almost every aspect of what he had learned from Sedgwick, and what he had taught himself that summer, in the Welsh Borderland and North Wales. These included the direct transect line across country, the inspection of sections and exposures, the marking of stratification on a map, the collection of rock specimens, the use of a clinometer (an instrument for measuring the dip of

3. Adam Sedgwick by S. Cousins, after T. Phillips. Sedgwick taught the young Darwin most of his geology during two weeks in North Wales in the summer of 1831. *National Portrait Gallery*

strata), geological hammer and compass. The excursion provided experience of dealing with innkeepers, of travel in wild places, sometimes under poor weather conditions – indeed of conducting a full fieldwork programme. Darwin, therefore, had good cause to write to Professor Henslow on 11 April 1833, just after he had left the Falkland Islands in the South Atlantic, asking him to tell Professor Sedgwick the he had 'never ceased to be thankful for that short tour in Wales'.

This instruction provided the basis for much of Darwin's geological work while he was on the *Beagle* voyage. Some of the crates sent back from the ship included rock and fossil specimens. Sedgwick was able to view these, and he wrote to Darwin's family: 'He is doing admirably in S. America, & has already sent home a collection above all praise.' Darwin was ever-after grateful for this training and support.

Despite their long friendship, Sedgwick, like Henslow, refused to accept all the implications of Darwin's evolutionary ideas. Indeed he wrote in a most outspoken manner after the publication of *On the Origin of Species* in November 1859. In a long letter he wrote of how much he admired the:

> … great knowledge; store of facts; capital views of the correlations of various parts of nature; admirable hints about the diffusions, thro' wide regions, of nearly related organic beings …

that the book revealed, but that he had:

> … read your book with more pain than pleasure. Parts of it I admired greatly; parts of it I laughed at till my sides were almost sore; other parts I read with absolute sorrow, because I think them utterly false and mischievous – You have deserted – after a start in that tram-road of solid physical truth – the true path of induction …

It was the materialist nature of the theory of natural selection that distressed Sedgwick most fervently. His letter continued:

> There is a moral or metaphysical part of nature as well as a physical. A man who denies this is deep in the mire of folly.

It obviously grieved Sedgwick dearly to disagree with his friend and former student so fundamentally. He wrote in such a forthright way only because he felt that Darwin was 'a good-tempered & truth loving man', and one might add, because he knew and respected him so well. A happy reconciliation occurred when Darwin visited Cambridge for his son Francis's graduation in May 1870.

Adam Sedgwick was a most inspiring and brilliant lecturer and teacher; he pioneered field-teaching with students. Some of his excursions would be conducted on horseback. Troops of up to 70 undergraduates would go galloping across the Cambridgeshire countryside, listening, in the course of the day, to a number of lectures. The last was given from the roof of the great cathedral at Ely, from which an extensive view of the surrounding landscape could be obtained.

At one stage in his career Sedgwick declaimed: 'I cannot promise to teach you all geology, I can only fire your imaginations.' And so he did. He held the Chair of Geology for around 55 years (until his death), and his legacy was enormous, and in some ways it still continues.

The importance of networking while at university, and establishing a cohort of friends who will prove useful later in a career, is often stressed to young people going to university today. Indeed to some it is recommended that they cultivate such a group (and indeed keep notes on associates that may prove useful years later! This might be called 'making your own luck'). It is unlikely that the young Charles Darwin did anything like this self-consciously. Nevertheless, some of his contemporaries, those with whom he attended some of those slightly disreputable dinners, and in particular those who were interested in natural history, especially the collection of beetles, did come in very useful later. When he was collecting information for his theories, seeking specimens, and accumulating material for his books, he frequently made use of some of his erstwhile student contacts.

Thomas Campbell Eyton, a scion of a noted Shrewsbury family, who was at school and at university with Darwin, later became an amateur ornithologist and was a source of information to him in later years. In October 1855 Charles wrote to him:

Ah the good old times of Entomology. I have never enjoyed anything in Natural History so much since.

Another of his student companions on beetle-hunting expeditions into the Cambridgeshire countryside was Albert Way. Albert was later to be one of the founders of the Institute of Archaeology and was a distinguished Fellow of the Society of Antiquaries. Darwin wrote to him in 1860 to ask him questions on the history of the dray horse for his book on the *Variation of Animals and Plants Under Domestication*. But he added 'Eheu Eheu [sigh, sigh] the old Crux Major days are long past'; he was thinking back to the days when he sought *Panagaeus crux major* with his student friend.

Yet another Cambridge friend with whom he went searching for beetles was his second cousin William Darwin Fox. There is some evidence that young Fox (who later did become a Church of England clergyman) was slightly more systematic in his collection and study. He wrote to him frequently during the Cambridge years, and those immediately following, often mentioning entomology.

In one vacation he wrote from Shrewsbury:

I am dying by inches from not having someone to talk to about insects. ... I was not fully aware of your extreme value before I left Cambridge. I am constantly saying 'I do wish Fox was here.' (Charles Darwin to William Darwin Fox, 12 June 1828)

It seems very possible that the Fox contact helped to impart a certain amount of rigour and system into Darwin's ventures into entomology, about which he was sometimes somewhat self-effacing, and which sometimes was little more than collecting for accumulation's sake. Cousin Fox may have insisted on accurate identification and given him tips on techniques of collecting and preserving natural history specimens that were useful on the *Beagle*.

Charles Darwin, living his 'retired' life in Down House, after 1842, was heavily dependent on his correspondents. Fox, Eyton and many others of his contemporaries comprised an important core to the network of the relationships important to him in his later work.

One of the most pleasant incidents of Darwin's Cambridge career occurred in early May 1831: it was the arrival of a fine microscope. It was accompanied by an anonymous note:

> If Mr. Darwin will accept the accompanying Coddington's Microscope, it will give peculiar gratification to one who has long doubted whether Mr. Darwin's talents or his sincerity be more worthy of admiration, and who hopes that the instrument may in some measure facilitate those researches which he has hitherto so fondly and so successfully prosecuted.

Darwin wrote to his cousin William Fox rejoicing in this 'delightful piece of luck'. It was only many years later that Charles found that the donor was his contemporary at Cambridge, John Maurice Herbert, who was at St John's College while Darwin was at Christ's. St John's was Henslow's college, and Herbert was a member of Henslow's circle. He clearly had formed a good impression both of Darwin's abilities and pleasant nature. Perhaps it was through meeting him at Henslow's natural history soirées that he realized that Darwin was destined for great things scientifically, was a thoroughly decent person, but needed a bit of help along the way.

Darwin wrote to his benefactor nearly 40 years later:

> Do you remember giving me anonymously a microscope? I can hardly call to mind any event in my life which surprised and gratified me more. (Charles Darwin to John Herbert, 21 November 1872)

Charles Darwin thought that the years at Cambridge had been wasted. But another way of looking at those years was to see the extent to which so many of the experiences of the years 1828 to 1831 later proved of the utmost importance to him. The love of the logic of Euclid perhaps helped him later in his work on geology; the reading of Paley stressed the need to prepare a structured argument and gave him an understanding of how organisms are adapted to their environment; the soirées at Professor Henslow's house introduced him to a network of those interested in natural history, some of whom, years later, provided him with significant information; it was through Henslow that Darwin received the invitation to join the *Beagle*; Henslow also fostered his friendship with Sedgwick (as well as guiding his reading). Sedgwick provided training in field methods in North Wales. Another contact provided the mysterious microscope. It was incredible how it all worked out. Luck? Yes? But after Edinburgh he knew how to get the best out of himself. He took pains to meet people and to be agreeable to them; he read widely; on his own admission he knew how to study hard for a few weeks in order to pass exams. His optimistic, reasonably outgoing manner and his experience – despite the alleged company of 'low-minded young men', the 'jolly singing', the cards, the dinners, the 'huntin' and shootin'' set, the rather indifferent degree – enabled him to find a pathway that led ultimately to astonishing success.

5

The Offer and its Acceptance

It might never have happened at all. Charles Darwin had quite different plans for the months following his graduation.

During his last few months as an undergraduate at Christ's College, Cambridge, in the late spring and early summer of 1831, Charles Darwin's friend and teacher, Professor John Henslow, seems to have lent his protégé a copy of an English translation of Alexander von Humboldt's *Personal Narrative of a Voyage to the Equinoctial Regions of a New Continent, 1799–1804*. (Humboldt is sometimes described as the 'Father of Modern Geography'; Darwin was to take a copy of the *Narrative* with him on the *Beagle* voyage.) The book made an enormous impression on Darwin: he read it 'with care and profound interest'. It was perhaps partly from Humboldt that he got part of his sense of integration – of the complex of relationships that exist among climate, rocks, landforms, plant and animal life, and human activities – that can be seen in a great deal of Darwin's writing. He went on to say that it was Humboldt's book (along with Sir John Herschel's *Introduction to the Study of Natural Philosophy*) that imparted to him 'a burning zeal to add even the most humble contribution to the noble structure of natural science'. 'No one or a dozen books' influenced him as much as these two. In his *Autobiography*, he described how he 'copied out from Humboldt, long passages about Teneriffe, and read them aloud'.

Some of these 'readings' seem to have occurred during the course of trips into the Cambridgeshire countryside, with Professor Henslow, Richard Dawes (later the Dean of Hereford) and Marmaduke Ramsay (a Fellow of Jesus College), and other young dons 'of the same standing'. The young Darwin seems to have rather overwhelmed his older friends with his enthusiasm:

> I ... talked about the glories of Teneriffe [Darwin used this spelling], and some of the party declared that they would go there; but I think they were only half in earnest. I was, however, quite in earnest, and got an introduction to a merchant in London to enquire about ships ... (*Autobiography*)

His letters confirm his near-obsession with Humboldt's description of the Isle of Tenerife. In a letter to his sister Caroline, written from Cambridge on 28 April 1831:

> All the while I am writing now my head is running about the Tropics: in the morning I go and gaze at Palm trees in the hot-house and come home and read Humboldt: my enthusiasm is so great I cannot hardly [*sic*] sit still in my chair. Henslow & other Dons give us great credit for our plan: Henslow promises to cram me in geology. I will never be easy till I see the peak of Teneriffe [*sic*] and the great Dragon tree; ... I am working regularly at Spanish ... I have written myself into a Tropical glow. [In fact Tenerife is about four degrees north of the Tropic of Cancer.]

In a letter to his cousin, W. D. Fox, about two weeks later, he wrote: 'As for my Canary scheme, it is rash of you to ask questions: My other friends sincerely wish me there, I plague them so with talking about tropical scenery &c &c. Eyton [a contemporary of Darwin's, see Chapter 4, page 32] will go next summer, & I am learning Spainish [*sic*]. How I wish we could meet. You would soon be tired of the subject.'

He wrote more letters, of much the same sort, to his cousin from Shrewsbury in July and early August 1831, and also one back to his teacher John Henslow in Cambridge:

> All now for the Canaries. I wrote to Mr. Ramsay, a little information I got in town ... Passage 20£; ships touch & return during the months of June to February. But not seeing myself the Broker, the 2 most important questions remain unanswered, viz. whether it means June inclusive & how often they sail. I will find this out before very long. I hope you continue to fan your Canary ardor: I read and reread Humboldt: do you do the same, & I am sure nothing will prevent us seeing the Great Dragon tree.

4. Dragon Tree, Tenerife. From the *Atlas Piltaresque*, which accompanied Alexander von Hamboldt's *Personal Narrative*, the book that encouraged the young Darwin to travel.

Humboldt's description of the Tenerife dragon tree seems to have been a particularly powerful influence. It reads:

Although we were acquainted, from the narratives of so many travellers, with the dragon tree … we were not the less struck with its enormous magnitude. We were told, that the trunk of this tree, which is mentioned in several very ancient documents as marking the boundaries of a field, was as gigantic in the fifteenth century. Its height appeared to be about 50 or 60 feet; its circumference near the roots is 45 feet … The trunk has a great number of branches, which rise to form a candelabrum, and are terminated by tufts of leaves. [It] bears still every year both flowers and fruit. Its aspect feelingly recalls to mind 'the eternal youth of nature', which is an inexhaustible source of motion and life.

But Messrs Eyton, Dawes, Henslow, Fox and Ramsay did not have to put up with Charles Darwin's enthusiasm for the Island of Tenerife in general, and the dragon tree in particular (Marmaduke Ramsay had died by the end of July anyway), for, as Darwin himself later put it, the scheme was 'knocked on the head by the voyage of the *Beagle*'. Nevertheless, were it not for the fact of his 'reading and re-reading' of Humboldt in the spring and summer of 1831, Darwin might never have developed his enthusiasm for remote volcanic islands, weird plants, and the brilliant light of the tropics. He might not have spent as much of that summer learning some geology, or mugging up sufficient Spanish to be useful in South America.

Darwin returned from his geological peregrination through northern Wales (Chapter 4) to his home in Shrewsbury to find a letter from Henslow (dated 24 August 1831). After a line or two of reflection on Ramsay's death, Henslow continued:

> ... I shall hope to see you shortly fully expecting that you will eagerly catch the offer which is likely to be made you of a trip to Terra [*sic*] del Fuego & home by the East Indies – I have been asked by Peacock [a Fellow of Trinity College Cambridge, and a friend of Captain, later Admiral, Beaufort, the hydrographer] ... to recommend him a naturalist as companion to Capt Fitzroy employed by Government to survey the S. extremity of America – I have stated that I consider you to be the best qualified person I know of who is likely to undertake such a situation. ... Capt. F. wants a man ... more as a companion than a mere collector & would not take any one however good a naturalist who was not recommended to him likewise as a gentleman. ... [I]f you take plenty of Books with you, anything you please may be done – You will have ample opportunities to command – In short I suppose there never was a finer chance for a man of zeal and spirit. ... Don't put on any modest doubts or fears about your qualifications for I assure you I think you are the very man they are in search of – so conceive yourself to be tapped on the Shoulder by your Bum-Bailiff & affect^e friend

> J. S. Henslow.

> [A bum-bailiff was described as a bailiff who was close upon the debtor's back, and about to catch him from the rear!]

Professor Henslow enclosed a letter from Peacock giving a few more details, and offering further encouragement. Darwin was urged to write immediately to Captain Beaufort at the Admiralty if he wished to accept the offer.

The bare facts expressed in Henslow's letter conceal quite complex negotiations among Captains FitzRoy and Beaufort at the Admiralty in London, and George Peacock and John Henslow in Cambridge. Henslow had apparently briefly considered the appointment himself (it had initially been planned for two years), but his young wife looked so miserable that he declined. So too, had his brother-in-law, the Rev Leonard Jenyns: Jenyns had even gone so far as to start packing his clothes! It was serendipity indeed that the offer got to Darwin just after his training in geology in North Wales.

However, a major barrier in the way of Darwin's acceptance was his father, who was so opposed that initially, and very hurriedly, Charles wrote to Henslow (30 August 1831) declining the offer. Dr Darwin's objections were numerous: the voyage would make it difficult to settle down as a clergyman; Charles had no experience of seafaring; there was too little time to prepare (it was originally planned that the departure would be at the end of September, just a few weeks after the return from North Wales); the scheme was a wild one, and in view of the fact that the offer had been made to others, as none of them had accepted there must be 'some serious objection to the vessel of the expedition'. The whole scheme was 'a useless undertaking', Robert Darwin asserted.

Faced with these outbursts, Charles said he would 'not be comfortable' disobeying his father's 'strong advice against going'. Nevertheless there was still a glimmer of hope. Dr Darwin did not absolutely refuse to allow his son to join the expedition. But first thing on the day after writing to Henslow reluctantly declining the invitation, Charles rode over to Maer, home of Dr Darwin's brother-in-law Josiah Wedgwood and Charles's own cousins, carrying a letter from his father in which he sought Josiah's 'unbiased opinion on the subject'.

At Maer, Charles later wrote, 'everything soon bore a different appearance'. He found every member of the Wedgwood family very strongly on his side. Josiah wrote a detailed reply, answering every one of Dr Robert Darwin's objections.

Participating in the expedition would not 'be in any degree disreputable to his character as a clergyman … on the contrary the offer [should be thought] honorable to him' and the pursuit of natural history was very suitable for a clergyman.

Taking part in the expedition, far from being 'a wild scheme', was every bit as sensible as activities he might be involved in during the next two years if he stayed at home. It might enable him to 'acquire and strengthen habits of application'.

It would be highly unlikely that the Admiralty would send out a bad vessel on such an important expedition.

There was no reason that following the voyage the young Darwin would not settle, like many another sailor returned from the sea, into 'domestic and quiet habits'.

Although the voyage might not be of direct use to a potential clergyman, 'looking upon him as a man of enlarged curiosity, it affords him such an opportunity of seeing men and things as happens to few'.

Josiah Wedgwood was extremely prescient, and an extremely good judge of Charles's character. All the predictions were eventually proved accurate.

Josiah sent off his reply to Dr Darwin very early on 1 September, and Charles went out shooting. When he returned to The Mount that evening, Darwin later wrote, 'all things were settled, & my Father most kindly gave his consent', writing to thank his brother-in-law at once: 'Charles has stated my objections quite fairly & fully – if he continues in the same mind after further enquiry, I will give him all the assistance in my power.' And so he did.

The same evening Charles wrote to Francis Beaufort at the Admiralty:

Shrewsbury
September the 1st.

Sir

I take the liberty of writing to you according to Mr Peacock's desire to aquaint you with my acceptance of the offer of going with Capt Fitzroy. Perhaps you may have received a letter from Mr Peacock, stating my refusal; this was owing to my Father not at first approving the plan, since which time he has reconsidered the subject: &

has given his consent & therefore if the appointment is not already filled up, – I shall be happy to have the honor of accepting it. ... I set out for Cambridge tomorrow morning, to see Professor Henslow: & from thence will proceed immediately to London.

I remain Sir, Your humble and obedient servant Chas. Darwin.

Beaufort passed the letter to FitzRoy, who minuted: 'Let him be borne on the books for vituals only.'

What a difference 36 hours can make!

Even so, it was, as Charles put it in a letter to his sister Susan a couple of days later, 'by no means' all settled. He told her to not to tell anyone in Shropshire of his plans, in case they fell through. Long discussions with Henslow, and interviews with FitzRoy and Beaufort still lay ahead.

The third day of September Darwin spent almost entirely with Professor Henslow in Cambridge, getting further information on Captain Robert FitzRoy, obtaining introductions to people in London who might assist him, and getting advice on collecting specimens and making observations. Darwin was also given good advice on luggage, oft-times unheeded by travellers before and since:

Henslow is much against taking too many things; it is a mistake all young travellers fall into. (Charles Darwin to Susan Darwin, 4 September 1831)

The next few days Darwin spent in London, in a series of meetings with FitzRoy and Beaufort, and making enquires about, and purchasing, the scientific equipment he needed for the voyage, to some extent under FitzRoy's supervision. The two men got on well. Darwin wrote to Henslow: 'Cap. FitzRoy is everything that is delightful ... I think he really wishes to have me.' He had perfect manners and Darwin felt it would be his own fault if they did not get on well. To his sister he reported that FitzRoy was his 'beau ideal of a Captain'. Nevertheless, FitzRoy cautioned him that quarters would be cramped, and catering arrangements fairly spartan.

A few days later Darwin went down to Plymouth to see the ship itself. There was a good deal of gallivanting around the country as Darwin returned to London at least twice, to purchase equipment (guns, nets, scientific instruments, storage for specimens and chemicals for preserving them, books), and then again visited Henslow in Cambridge, to receive further advice. There was a goodbye visit to Shrewsbury (and Maer) in late September. And then down to Devonport, where he stayed, somewhat frustratedly, for several weeks while the ship was being prepared. A note in a letter from Devonport to John Henslow dated 30 October 1831 is interesting, saying something as it does about both their characters:

> What an important Epoch 1831 will be in my life, taking one degree, & starting for Patagonia are each in their respective ways remarkable events. – And you have been most instrumental in getting them both. – Remember me most kindly to Mrs Henslow. – Leonard Jenyns & all other friends. – I often think of your good advice of taking all uncomfortable moments as a matter of course, & not to be compared with all the lasting & solid advantages: – Indeed I never can do better than when I think of you & your advice.

'Uncomfortable moments' abounded in the weeks, months and years that followed, and Charles probably reflected on this advice frequently. His optimism and determination carried him through, as he reflected on the lasting and solid advantages that lay ahead.

The planned late September date for sailing was long past and September had given way to October. A date in November was fixed, and then abandoned. There was 'delay after delay', partly due to inclement weather, partly due to work still needing to be done on the ship. December approached. Brother Erasmus arrived in Devonport on 2 December to see him off. The sixth of December was fixed for departure, but on that day Darwin wrote in his diary 'Again sailing has been deferred', and he dined that evening with his brother. The ship departed on 9 December, Erasmus going as far as the breakwater. But a heavy gale came from the south-west and Darwin 'suffered most dreadfully' and 'it was determined to put back to Plymouth'. A further few weeks of languishing in harbour followed. On 19 December he noted hopefully: 'There is every probability of sailing tomorrow morning. The weighing of our anchor will be hailed with universal joy.' But it was not to be. A strong south-west wind blew in torrents of rain. Christmas Day and then Boxing Day came and went. The latter was 'a beautiful day & and excellent one for sailing' but departure had yet again to be postponed due to the 'drunkenness and absence of nearly the whole crew'. Many were flogged or confined to chains for many hours.

It was not until 11.00 a.m. on 27 December that the 'long wished for wind from the east' came, and they weighed anchor. Darwin and Lieutenant Sulivan lunched on mutton chops and champagne, which, it was felt, might excuse 'the total absence of sentiment' he felt on leaving England.

Had not Darwin and his friends toyed with the idea of an expedition in Humboldt's footsteps to Tenerife, Charles might not have spent the summer of 1831 learning Spanish. Had not Henslow suggested geological studies, and the Sedgwick expedition honed his geological skills, Darwin would have been less well prepared than he was for the voyage.

Had FitzRoy not approached Beaufort in his request for a 'savant' to attend to the natural history of the voyage, or Beaufort exploited the Cambridge network though his friend Peacock, or some other contact decided to accept the invitation, or had Charles and the Wedgwood family not been able to win round Dr Robert Darwin in his objections to 'a wild scheme', things might have been very different. The chain might have been broken at any point, and the young 'unfinished naturalist', so obviously suitable in the eyes of both Professor Henslow and Josiah Wedgwood, would never have got his opportunity. Simple chance played an important role. But Charles Darwin's optimism, determination, and his ability, encouraged by Henslow, to endure temporary discomforts and setbacks for long-term advantages, helped him to 'make his own luck'.

6

Sailor's Luck

Darwin had a specially warm relationship with his sister Caroline, and several times in her letters to him over the five years he was aboard the *Beagle* she wrote to him of her concern over the dangers he faced, both on land and at sea. On 27 April 1832 she wrote to him a letter full of sisterly love:

> I wish I could be sure of your escaping all the innumerable ... dangers you are exposed to. For Heaven's sake take care of yourself, is all I entreat of you. ... I am sure prudence must do a great deal in saving people from risks and dangers, and my hope is in your sense saving you.

Charles Darwin did not take too many unnecessary risks, although as a young man he sometimes left no stone unturned to collect a particular rock specimen or to gain a view from a high point. Occasionally one can detect a degree of impetuousness as he records in his diary or notes crashing through the undergrowth on a mountainside, using a 'jumping pole' to access coral reefs some distance from the shore, or experimenting on himself to discover the effects of stinging creatures, dodging a firefight in South America, or in his association with gauchos, some of whom had a reputation for being extremely bloodthirsty!

One of his other sisters expressed herself in a heartfelt manner when, after the family had received part of Charles's diary, Susan wrote on 22 November 1835:

> Papa enjoys it extremely except when the dangers you run makes him shudder: Indeed I think the escapes you have had of different dangers are quite providential!

The young naturalist was seldom reckless, but often extremely determined. He took risks, and knew it. But his determination was balanced by caution. He was an experienced horseman, quite a good shot, and he knew his capabilities. On his land expeditions he was adequately equipped. Nevertheless he was extremely fortunate in the seamanship of HMS *Beagle's* crew, particularly Robert FitzRoy the captain, and the officers such as Lieutenants Bartholomew Sulivan and John Wickham, and Acting Surgeon Benjamin Bynoe, both during the voyage and prior to it. FitzRoy had insisted on modifications to the ship, raising the deck by some inches, and made sure that the boat was extremely well equipped with navigational instruments. These precautions almost certainly saved the lives of the ship's company. Nevertheless, were it not for, as Susan Darwin put it, 'providence', or good fortune, fate or luck, the outcome might have been very different.

HMS *Beagle*, with the eager young naturalist aboard, left Plymouth two days after Christmas 1831 (he had been living aboard for some weeks). For the first few weeks of the voyage (and frequently thereafter) Darwin was extremely seasick. However, his first flirtation with real danger seems to have come at St Paul's Rocks. Late on 15 February 1832, the ship's company of the *Beagle* 'Saw the rocks of St Paul's right ahead'. The vessel hove to for the night. On the sixteenth they moved a little closer, and when three miles distant boats were lowered, one with a surveying party led by Lieutenant Stokes, and one with Lieutenant Wickham and Darwin 'for geologising & shooting'.

St Paul's are a tiny cluster of rocks almost on the Equator (in fact 0° 58'N, 29°15'W). The islet is 540 miles (870km) from the coast of South America. The highest point is about 60 feet (18.3 metres) above sea level, and the circumference of the little group is only three quarters of a mile (about 2km). Darwin and his shipmates had seen large flocks of seabirds soaring above the islands, and noticed the brilliant white appearance of the bird droppings on the rocks. The boats had great difficulty in landing 'as the long swell of the open sea broke with violence on the rocky coast', and the rocks were in places very steep. But on landing a 'most extraordinary' sight was presented to them. They were surrounded on all sides by birds that were 'so unaccustomed to men that they would not move'. Many were knocked down with stones and by Darwin's geological hammer.

'Shooting was out of the question [Darwin wrote], so we got two of the boat's crew & the work of slaughter commenced.' They collected a pile of birds, and hatfuls of eggs, and Darwin obtained some rock specimens, which he did not fully understand, but he appreciated that they were not volcanic, as were the rocks of many remote islands (they are now known to be of eclogite, from deep within the earth).

> While we were so active on shore, the men in the boat were not less so. They caught a great number of fine large fish & would have succeeded much better had not the sharks broken so many of their hooks and lines: they contrived to land three of these latter fish, & during our absence 2 large ones were caught from the ship.

FitzRoy described the scene even more vividly:

> While our party were scrambling over the rock, a determined struggle was going on in the water, between the boats' crews and sharks. Numbers of fine fish, like the groupars (or garoupas) of the Bermuda Islands, bit eagerly at baited hooks … but as soon as a fish was caught, a rush of voracious sharks was made at him, and notwithstanding blows of oars and boat hooks, the ravenous monsters could not be deterred from seizing and taking away more than half the fish that were hooked. (R. FitzRoy, *Narrative of the Surveying Voyage*)

The task of getting back into the boats and away was no doubt made all the more difficult by the fact that at the end of the day they were 'a good deal fatigued', and also exhausted by the 'glaring heat' reflected from the brilliantly white rocks, very close to the Equator. The fact that several men (some of them inexperienced and unaccustomed to the tropical heat) were able to get ashore on this tiny group of steep rocks pounded by Atlantic breakers, with sharks awaiting any unfortunate who fell overboard, to spend several hours collecting rock specimens, and birds and eggs for food, and then bringing them back to the ship, is noteworthy. Darwin makes light of it but he must at times have been frightened.

HMS *Beagle* spent the next Christmas, that of 1832, at Wigwam Cove, on Hermit Island, a few miles to the west of Cape Horn. Duties were suspended and after breakfast, Darwin, Lieutenant Sulivan and Midshipman Hamond climbed Kater's Peak, rising to 1,700 feet (about 550m), but the trip was recreational rather than scientific. Sulivan amused himself by rolling large stones down the precipices; Darwin hammered rather unsystematically on the rocks; they screamed out merrily to hear the echoes. Some of the ship's company, high-spiritedly, fired gunshots into caverns at wildfowl (this sounds rather dangerous). On a date close to the longest day of the year, at 56°S the sun set late, but as it did so, the sky looked 'ominous'. During the following night 'it blew a tremendous gale'. On 26 December it remained 'unsettled & most exceedingly unpleasant'. On the 27th, 28th and 29th Darwin recorded in his diary that it was 'very bad with much rain and violent squalls' and that it was 'bleak & raw'.

On New Year's Eve there was sunshine and 'the weather did not look quite so bad' and they put to sea. But the good fortune was short-lived. On 1 January it blew a strong gale from the south-west. The blow continued for several days and on 3 January Darwin wrote that 'after four days we have scarcely gained a league'. His diary entries for 4 to 12 January 1832 are littered with phrases such as 'beating day and night against the Westerly winds', 'slow progress', 'it blew strong', 'strong gale', 'ship heavily pitching', 'miseries of constant cold & wet', 'scarcely an hour free from sea-sickness', 'violent squall', 'regular storm'. On the eighth the ship drifted south to 57°23'S. Darwin noted on one occasion: 'To give an idea of the fury of the unbroken ocean, clouds of spray were carried over a precipice which must have been 200 feet (65m) high'. At times however, they did not know where they were.

On the morning of 13 January, he was clearly anxious; he wrote:

> The gale does not abate: if the Beagle was not an excellent sea-boat & our tackle in good condition, we should be in distress. A less[er] gale has dismasted & foundered many a good ship.

Yet even in such circumstances the naturalist was observing: 'it was curious', he noted, 'to see how the Albatross with its widely expanded wings, glided right up the wind.'

The Captain now takes up the account.

At three in the morning on the 13th, the vessel lurched so deeply and the mast bent and quivered so much, that I reluctantly took in the main-sail (small as it was when close reefed), leaving only the storm trysails (close reefed) and fore-staysails. At ten, there was so continued and heavy a rush of wind, that even the diminutive trysails oppressed the vessel too much and they were still further reduced. ... Soon after one the sea had risen to a great height and I was anxiously watching the successive waves, when three huge rollers approached, whose size and steepness at once told me that our sea-boat, good as she was, would be *sorely tried*. Having steerage way, the vessel met and rose over the first unharmed, but of course her way was checked; the second deadened her way completely, throwing her off wind; and the third great sea, taking her right abeam, turned her so far over, that all the lee bulwarks, from the cat-head to the stern davit were two or three feet under water.

For a moment our position was critical, but like a cask, she rolled back again, though with some feet of water over the whole deck. Had another sea struck her, the little ship might have been numbered among the many of her class which have disappeared, but the crisis was past. She shook the sea off her through the ports and was none the worse – excepting the loss of the lee-quarter boat, which although carried three feet higher than in the former voyage [because, at Captain FitzRoy's insistence, the deck had been raised during refitting in Plymouth a year before], was dipped under water and torn away.

Darwin confirms most of these details, although he suggests that the boat had to be deliberately cut adrift:

At noon the storm was at its height; & we began to suffer; a great sea struck & came on board; the after tackle of the quarter boat gave way & an axe being obtained they were instantly obliged to cut away one of the beautiful whale boats; the same sea filled our decks so deep, that if another had followed it is not difficult to imagine the result. It is not easy to imagine what a state of confusion the decks were in from the great body of water. At last the ports were knocked open & she again rose buoyant in the sea.

He also grumbled that his drying paper and some of his plant specimens had been soaked. He reported that FitzRoy had described the storm as 'the worst he was ever in'.

Yet even these two accounts may not give quite the full story. In his own memoirs Bartholomew Sulivan recalled that Captain FitzRoy always had

5. 'Sorely tried' by John Chancellor. Painting of HMS *Beagle* in bad weather, south of Cape Horn. *Published with the kind permission of the artist's son, Gordon Chancellor*

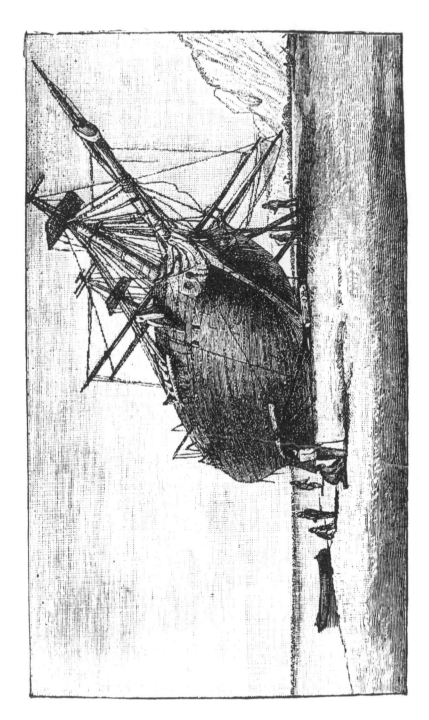

6. HMS *Beagle* ashore in South America. *From Captain Robert FitzRoy's Narrative of a Surveying Voyage*

the ports (the openings through which deck water could run off) secured. Lieutenant Sulivan was not happy with this and instructed the carpenter to always have a handspike to hand in case of emergencies. Sulivan was on deck shortly before the great seas struck, but relinquished to FitzRoy. But on returning to the deck, he found the carpenter waist-deep in water, attempting to drive a handspike against the port; this eventually burst open releasing the water. It was thus Sulivan's foresightedness that saved the day. FitzRoy, in his official account, may have glossed over this detail as well as the fact that one of the boats had to be cut away.

Just over a fortnight later (on 29 January 1833), FitzRoy, Darwin and a few others took two of the ship's boats to explore the Beagle Channel. The scenery was 'very grand', with lofty mountains 'covered with a white mantle of perpetual snow'. Waterfalls tumbled into the Channel, and 'beryl blue' glaciers reached the water's edge. While having a meal in a small bay and admiring the beautiful colours of the 'vertical and overhanging face' of one of these glaciers, 'a large mass fell roaring into the water'. Darwin continues:

> Our boats were on the beach; we saw a great wave rushing onwards, & instantly it was evident how great was the chance of their being dashed to pieces. One of the seamen just got hold of the boat as the curling breaker reached it: he was knocked over & over but not hurt & most fortunately our boat received no damage. If they had been washed away, how dangerous would our lot have been, surrounded on all sides by hostile savages & deprived of all provisions.

Darwin modestly slightly understates the situation. FitzRoy's account says there was a 'thundering crash' and that it was 'the whole front of the icy cliff' that tumbled down, and

> the sea surged up in a vast heap of foam. Reverberating echoes sounded in every direction … but our whole attention was immediately called to great rolling waves which came so rapidly that there was scarcely time for the most active of our party to run and seize the boats before they were tossed along the beach like empty calabashes. By the exertions of those who grappled them or seized the ropes they were hauled out of reach of a second and third roller. … [T]hey were just saved in time, for had not Mr Darwin, and two or three of the men, run to them instantly, they would have been swept away irrecoverably.

7. The Beagle Channel, Tierra del Fuego. *Photo by author*

The following day FitzRoy named a nearby mountain Mount Darwin to commemorate the incident and express his appreciation for his 'messmate who so willingly encountered the discomfort and risk of a long cruise in a small loaded boat'.

All manner of dangers lurked in those southern waters. A very few weeks later, on 4 March 1833, Mr E. H. Hellyer, Captain FitzRoy's clerk, drowned, becoming entangled in the fronds of kelp, near Port Louis, East Falkland. He had been walking along the shore of Berkeley Sound, and seeing a species of duck he had not seen previously, shot it, and waded into the water to recover the specimen. FitzRoy recalled in his *Narrative*:

> Being alone, and finding the water cold, he may have been alarmed, then accidentally entangling his legs in the sea-weed, lost his presence of mind, and by struggling hastily was only more confused. The rising tide must have considerably augmented his distress, and hastened the fatal result.

Darwin was close by and seems to have been a member of the recovery party. The body was 'not many yards from the shore but so entangled in Kelp that is was with difficulty disengaged'. Darwin made a detailed study of the ecological links within the kelp-bed ecosystem, and almost certainly waded out to collect specimens. Bearing in mind the fate of Hellyer – who was buried on a lonely headland the next day – the young naturalist was in some danger. Good fortune and his own caution preserved him.

Darwin was quite seriously ill several times during the course of the voyage. On 2 October 1832, while riding, in Argentina, between Buenos Aires and Santa Fe, he seems to have suffered from heatstroke. He felt 'Unwell & feverish, from having exerted myself too much in the sun. … I was much exhausted'. He was 'Unwell in bed' for the next two days, and although he was on the move again shortly after, he describes himself as 'Not quite well'.

More serious were the effects of what may have been some kind of food poisoning, which he experienced in Chile, in September 1834. He had visited some gold mines and whilst there, 'drank some Chichi, a very weak, sour new made wine'. (*Chicha* is still made in some parts of Chile: it is described as a sweet wine with a high alcohol content; perhaps there was something wrong with the refreshments served at those gold mines!) This, he thought, was the cause of his disordered stomach, the terrible weakness he felt, and his completely lost appetite, all of which laid him low for several weeks. He was in bed for a month, and seems to have been very ill indeed. The *Beagle's* surgeon, Benjamin Bynoe, visited him (by this time Darwin was staying in a house in Valparaiso), and prescribed rest and 'a good deal of calomel'. Calomel is mercury chloride (Hg_2Cl_2) a dense white or yellowish, odourless solid which was, in the middle years of the nineteenth century, widely given as a diuretic or purgative. However, its use for this purpose has long since been abandoned because of its very toxic nature: even if Darwin had not been at risk from food poisoning, he was at very real risk of the poisonous effects of the mercury. The cure might, had it not been for Darwin's luck, have proven worse than the disease!

Even more serious could have been the bites he received, possibly on several occasions, from a bug, *Triatoma infestans* (Heteroptera). The best

8. Kelp bed, East Falkland. One of Darwin's shipmates drowned while obtaining history specimens from such a tangled forest of seaweed. *Photo by author*

documented instance was on about 26 March 1835, near Mendoza, western Argentina, in the foothills of the Andes:

> At night I experienced an attack, & it deserves no less a name, of the Benchuca, the great black bug of the Pampas. It is most disgusting to feel soft wingless insects, about an inch long, crawling over one's body; before sucking; they are quite thin, but afterwards round & bloated with blood, & in this state they are easily squashed. They are also found in the Northern part of Chili & in Peru: one which I caught at Iquiqui [Iquique was not visited until July 1835] was very empty; being placed on a Table & though surrounded by people, if a finger was presented, its sucker was withdrawn, & the bold insect began to drawn blood. It was curious to watch the change in the size of the insect's body in less than ten minutes. There was no pain felt. This one meal kept the insect fat for four months; in a fortnight, however, it was ready, if allowed, to suck more blood. (*Diary*, 25–6 March 1835, but obviously written up much later.)

Eventually, after keeping the creature for some four and a half months, Darwin killed it to retain as a specimen, but it has been lost. This insect is the vector of a protozoan parasite (*Trypanosoma cruzi*), which enters the body though broken skin. The insects often defecate during their bloody meal, and it is from the faeces that the organism of infection may enter the body, causing American trypanosomiasis or Chagas' disease. It is sometimes maintained that the ill health that Darwin experienced in his later life was due to this infection. However, although Darwin was at very real risk of catching this disease, the evidence that he actually did is not strong. One of the symptoms is a swelling of the eyelids; another is swollen lymph nodes. Darwin does not mention anything of this nature. Moreover, although the disease can remain in the system without there being any visible symptoms for months or years, victims often present with severe cardiac problems, and frequently do not survive to the age Darwin reached. Exceptions occur, however. One possibility might be that Darwin was infected, but the disease did not develop to its full extent in him.

But there were dangers from animals a good deal larger than insects and protozoa. On 17 March 1834 (St Patrick's Day), Darwin was heading westwards, on horseback across East Falkland, on his second visit to these islands.

9. Stone-run on East Falkland. The landscape of the Falkland Islands is covered by these glacier-like streams of stones. They constitute a major impediment to travel on horseback and an inconvenience when on foot. *Photo by author*

Cattle were numerous, but because of the recent slaughter of cows, bulls were in the majority. These feral animals (the descendants of those introduced some decades earlier) were not to be trifled with.

> These [bulls] wander about in twos & threes or by themselves & are very savage. I never saw such magnificent beasts; they truly resemble ancient sculptures, in which the vast head and neck is but seldom seen in tame animals. The young bulls run away for a short distance, but the old ones will not stir a step excepting to rush a man & horse; & many horses have thus been killed. One old bull crossed a boggy stream & took up his stand on the side opposite to us. We in vain tried to drive him away & failing we were obliged to make a large circuit.

Taking considerable risks, Darwin's companions had their own back:

> Gauchos in revenge were determined to render him for the future innocuous [i.e. castrate him]; it was very interesting to see art completely mastered such huge force. One lazo was thrown over his horns as he rushed at the horse, & another round his hind legs; in a minute the monster was stretched harmless on the ground.

Had his companions not known their business extremely well, Darwin, or one or more of the gauchos, might have been badly gored.

Horseback travel in the Falklands posed other dangers; the countryside is traversed by stone-runs, glacier-like streams, up to 2 miles (3km) in length, of irregularly shaped rocks. These are almost impossible to cross on horseback, and pose difficulties to those on foot.

The long voyage across the Pacific, with its visits to the Galapagos, Tahiti, New Zealand and Australia was not without incident – he nearly ran out of water and food while ashore in the Galapagos, and the seasickness was a constant problem, but the extreme weather of the southern tip of South America and its adjacent islands was behind them.

But then there was the incident of the poisonous fish. In the first week of April 1836, following calls at the Australian ports of Sydney, Hobart Town and King George's Sound, the *Beagle* visited the Cocos Islands in the Indian Ocean. There he collected a common fish, named *Scarus chlorodon* by Leonard Jenyns in *The Zoology of the Voyage of the Beagle* volume on Darwin's collection of fishes, a species which fed exclusively on coral. There

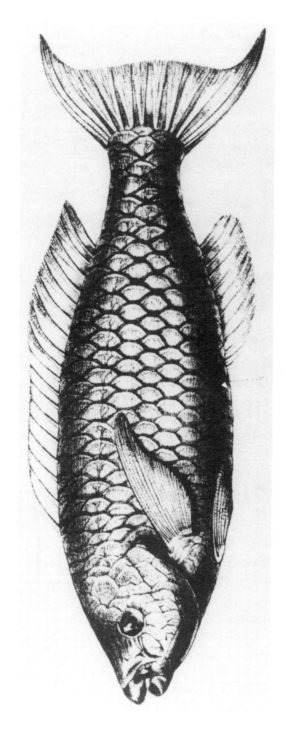

10. Parrottfish from the Cocos (Keeling) Islands, Indian Ocean. Fish of this genus have been found to be poisonous. If Darwin ate some – and he may have – he was in real danger. *From an illustration in the Fish volume (iv) of* The Zoology of the Voyage of the Beagle

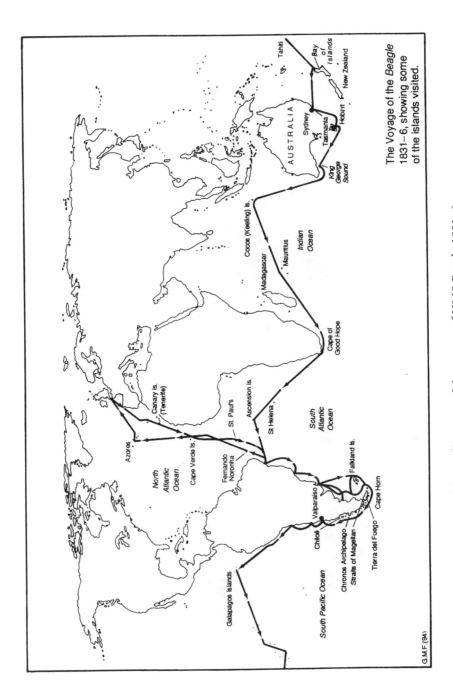

11. Outline map of the voyage of HMS *Beagle*, 1831–6

were two species of these fish, both with strong bony jaws, and both 'coloured a splendid bluish-green': one lived in the lagoon, another among the corals of the outer breakers. Darwin, ever interested in the relationships between an organism and its environment, opened the intestines of several of these 'parrotfishes' (the modern scientific name of one species that he collected is *Scarus prasiognathos*), and found them distended with 'yellow calcareous sandy mud'. The flesh of some species in this genus is on occasion very poisonous; there is evidence that Darwin ate some – if so he was in very real danger. *Ciguatera* is the name given to the form of toxicity derived from the eating of fish containing toxins produced by a micro-organism, the dinoflagellate *Gambierdiscus toxicus*.

From the Cocos the *Beagle* proceeded to Mauritius and the Cape of Good Hope. From there she went on to the islands of St Helena and Ascension and then, touching briefly on the mainland of South America again, continued via the Cape Verde Islands and the Azores, reaching Falmouth, in south-west England, on a stormy night on 2 October 1836. From there Darwin dashed, by a series of stagecoaches through the autumn days and nights, to his family awaiting him anxiously in Shrewsbury.

7

Scientific Development aboard HMS Beagle: *Seeing Things in the Right Order*

We have seen how it was that, by normal standards of evaluation, Charles Darwin's time as a medical student was a miserable failure: he hated the sight of blood, found the experience of watching operations being performed (without anaesthetic) utterly horrific, and the lectures boring. He left Edinburgh unqualified. Yet, young as he was, he benefited from the association with Dr Grant, exploring the intellectual recesses of the city with his brother Erasmus, listening to papers being delivered at the Plinian Society, delivering papers himself, taking part in scientific discussion and indeed witnessing scientific and philosophical controversy in all its fury (see Chapter 3). Edinburgh taught Darwin how to learn. Moreover, despite his disgust at medical training, we have also seen that there are many signs in his writings from later life that he absorbed a good deal of it.

While the Cambridge years were punctuated by a good deal of feasting, socializing and shooting, the contacts he made there led to the *Beagle* voyage invitation, and the building up of a network of friends who were to be of use to him throughout his career. No experience was wasted: everything could be turned to good account.

The serendipity continued. In the spring and summer of 1831, while Charles was contemplating a career in the Church, and the life of a country rector, having read Humboldt's accounts, he planned an expedition to Tenerife, pestering several of his Cambridge friends with enthusiastic letters on the subject – a final frolic before settling into a country parish, perhaps. With this project in view he taught himself some geology, he went on the geological field excursion to North Wales with Adam Sedgwick, and learned a smattering of Spanish. The expedition to Tenerife never took place; one of the proposed expeditioners, Marmaduke Ramsay, had died by the end of the summer, and some of the others were probably not very serious about the proposal. (Although the *Beagle* included Tenerife in her itinerary, quarantine restrictions prevented Darwin from landing, to his enormous disappointment.) But the planning, the mugging up of geology, the field training with Sedgwick, the development of an enthusiasm for remote islands (and reading about them), learning some basic Spanish, meant that from early in the voyage the young naturalist was able to 'hit the ground running'.

One of the ironies of the history of science is that it was Captain Robert FitzRoy, commander of HMS *Beagle* on her 1831–6 voyage, who gave Darwin his copy of the first volume of Charles Lyell's *Principles of Geology* on the eve of departure. The book still exists, with the Captain's friendly handwritten inscription. FitzRoy later became a fierce opponent of Darwin's evolutionary ideas, yet Lyell's work (of which volumes two and three reached Darwin while he was in South America) advocates the doctrine of uniformitarianism, the notion that the earth's geological features are best understood in terms of the long-continued action of very slow processes that can be seen at work today. Lyell makes a good deal of the role of uplift and subsidence in the development of the features of the earth's surface, as well as the importance of volcanic activity. These ideas profoundly influenced Darwin during the voyage, and were among a range of influences that ultimately steered him towards his evolutionary notions.

Because of the excitements of departure, and being dreadfully seasick for much of the first few days, Darwin probably did not read much of Lyell until the voyage was a few weeks old. But he may have glanced at it, and extracted the notion of the continual change that has affected the earth.

On 3 January he recorded:

We looked for the eight stones & passed over the spot where they are laid down on the charts. Perhaps their origin might have been Volcanic & [they] have since disappeared. (*Diary*)

Captain FitzRoy, with his experienced mariner's practicality, rather than the philosopher's speculative approach, was convinced, after a thorough searching, that the 'Eight Stones' did not exist. He wrote:

> On the 3d of January we were occupied in looking for the 'Eight Stones'; but nothing was seen to indicate either rocks, or shoals or even shallow water. The sun was shining brightly on a deep blue sea, of one uniform colour: no soundings could be obtained; and had there been a shoal or a rock within seven miles of us at any hour of that day, it could not have passed unnoticed. So many vessels have searched, in vain, for this alleged group of rocks, that their existence can now hardly be thought possible. (*Narrative of the Surveying Voyages of His Majesty's Ships Adventure and Beagle.* Vol 2, London: Henry Colburn, 1839)

Disappearing islands have long been part of the lore of the sea. A glimpse of a distant breaking wave; in higher latitudes, a far-travelled iceberg, particularly if it carries a good deal of dark, eroded rocky material; or perhaps even a whale or some other form of marine life when seen under certain light conditions have initiated reports of isolated islets or lonely rocks. Occasionally, of course, such a distant glimpse might have been gained through the cloudy mist of the contents of a bottle of rum! Such reports often found their way into 'Instructions for Mariners' or onto Admiralty charts. In the interests of safety, they might remain there for decades, long after it had become clear to some mariners that they did not exist.

Yet volcanic islands *do* come and go. Suddenly they emerge from the sea, expand, throwing out lava and ash for months or even years, but eventually the friable volcanic material is eroded by the waves, or the whole structure subsides, collapsing into a magma chamber beneath, and the island is submerged. A volcanic explanation for the origin and disappearance of the Eight Stones is not completely impossible: shallow areas of sea do exist north of Madeira, and there are clear records of volcanic islets in the vicinity of the Azores – not too far distant – appearing and disappearing within a few months, once or twice during the nineteenth century.

Whatever the true explanation for the origin and disappearance of the mysterious Eight Stones, the fact that Darwin thought that they might be volcanic is perhaps significant. Darwin was, later in the voyage, to embrace

Lyell's uniformitarian views more firmly, but it is of note that just a week into the voyage he was speculating that islands might appear and disappear through the action of natural geological processes, and thus appreciating, early on, that he lived in a changing, dynamic world.

The Eight Stones had disappeared (if they ever existed); Darwin had been too sick to leave his hammock as they passed Madeira, and landing on Tenerife had been banned by the quarantine authorities. He half-consoled himself with the thought that tropical islands must be rather alike. But they landed on St Jago (São Tiago), in the Cape Verde Islands a few days later and his luck turned.

He had been told by some of his shipmates that it was a miserable place, and his initial impression was unfavourable; the people of the Porto Praya lived in a state of 'degradation'; the land was 'sterile' because of the desert climate. But he left the town behind, and entered one of the deep valleys that have been cut into the dry plateau surface. The effect was almost stupefying:

> Here I first saw the glory of tropical vegetation: Tamarinds, Bananas and Palms were flourishing at my feet … It is not only the gracefulness of their forms or the novel richness of their colours, it is the numberless & confused associations that rush together on the mind, & produce the effect. I returned to the shore, treading on Volcanic rocks, hearing the notes of unknown birds, & seeing new insects fluttering about still newer flowers. It has been for me a glorious day, like giving to a blind man eyes, he is overwhelmed with what he sees & cannot justly comprehend it. Such are my feelings, & such may they remain. (*Diary*, 17 January 1832)

Figure 12 shows the striking contrast between the incised valleys on St Jago, and the arid surrounding plateau. The photo shows a valley close to the one Darwin explored: the one he actually examined is now affected by urban development. The stark comparison between the two environments comes through clearly in his descriptions – the habit of comparison was fundamental to his method of observation.

Darwin spent much of the next couple of days on Quail Island (now Ilheu Santa Maria), where Captain FitzRoy had established a sort of tented observation centre, from which to make navigational, magnetic and astronomical measurements (this was one of the *Beagle* expedition's principal

12. Valley on the Island of St Jago, Cape Verde Islands. The actual valley described by Darwin in his diary has been affected by development. This nearby valley is very similar. Note the striking contrast between the bare plateau surface and the vegetated valley. *Photo by author*

duties). Darwin carefully examined the volcanic rocks, and also the marine organisms that he found along the rocky shore. The sense of excitement remained:

> The first examining of Volcanic rocks, must to a Geologist be a memorable epoch, & little less so to the naturalist is the first burst of admiration at seeing Corals growing on their native rock. Often whilst in Edinburgh, have I gazed at the little pools of water left by the tide: & from the minute corals on our own shore pictured to myself those of larger growth: little did I think how exquisite their beauty is & still less did I expect my hopes of seeing them would ever be realised.
>
> The investigation of the geology of all the places visited was far more important than natural history, as reasoning here comes into play. On first examining a new district nothing can appear more hopeless than the chaos of rocks; but by recording the stratification and nature of rocks and fossils at many points, always reasoning and predicting what will be found elsewhere, light soon begins to dawn ... and the structure of the whole becomes more or less intelligible. (*Autobiography*)

Detailed observation, comparison of one place with another, and logical reasoning: Darwin took to field geology like a duck to water, and the little, desolate Quail Island was his nursery. He studied there the relationship of one rock-type to another, he found fossils and noted how they occurred in relation to each other:

> At Quail Island, the calcareous deposit is replaced in its lowest part by a soft, brown, earthy tuff, full of Turritelli: this is covered by a bed of pebbles, passing into sandstone, and mixed with fragments of echini, claws of crabs, and shells; the oyster-shells still adhering to the rock on which they grew. (C. Darwin, *Geological Observations on Volcanic Islands*, 1844, Chapter 1)

He noted the form of the landscape – the rounded volcanic cones, the craters, the cliffs, the different layers of rock in the valleys, the vivid contrast between the white limestone and the dark lava: and thus he was 'able to make out the geology of the district'.

Late in life he recalled how on tiny Quail Island – 'less than a mile in circumference' – and on the nearby main island, things suddenly 'came together' for him, geologically.

The geology of St. Jago is very striking yet simple: a stream of lava formerly flowed over the bed of the sea, formed of triurated recent shells and corals, which it has baked into a hard white rock. Since then the whole island has been upheaved. But the line of white rock revealed to me a new and important fact, namely that there had been afterwards subsidence round the craters, which had been in action, and poured forth lava. It then first dawned on me that I might perhaps write a book on the geology of the various countries visited, and this made me thrill with delight. That was a memorable hour to me, and how distinctly I can call to mind the low cliff of lava beneath which I rested, with the sun glowing hot, a few strange desert plants growing near, and with living corals in the tidal pools at my feet. (*Autobiography*)

As well as getting the feel for seeing in three dimensions, and appreciating that both rises and falls of the sea level in relation to the land had taken place at a not-too-far-distant geological time, Darwin was getting a feel for the span of time. There were the fossil corals, and close by, in the sea at the foot of the cliff, were the living forms.

Another ravine was different again; it had very steep rocky sides, about 30 yards across and with walls about 200 feet (60m) high:

In this wild dell we found the building places for several birds, Hawks & Ravens & the beautiful tropic birds were soaring about us: a large wild cat bounded across … The place seemed formed for wild animals: large blocks of rocks, entwined with succulent creepers & the ground strewn over with bleached bones of goats would have been a fine habitation for a Tiger.

There were also examples of that strange, giant tropical tree with the swollen trunk, the baobab, *Adansonia digitata*.

But fascinating as the plants and animals of St Jago were, it was, as he himself states, the geological phenomena that were of real importance to him: 'the geology is … very striking, yet simple'. The layers of limestone (Pliocene) and the overlying lava are almost horizontal – the limestone dips slightly to below sea level in places. The strata are clearly visible in the steep-sided valleys and along the eroded cliffs of the coast. Even when he ventured inland, the geology was plain to him, as there was no covering of vegetation to obscure it. Although he was not yet fully converted to Lyell's views, he had perhaps read enough to understand the importance of uplift and subsidence. The limestone with the fossils in it, so similar to the organisms of the modern beach, must have been uplifted: perhaps the movement was associated with the volcanic activity so evident on the island. The steep valleys must have been eroded by water (he was not certain how).

Although many have suggested that it was on Quail Island that the 'Eureka moment' occurred – the instant that he realized the significance of the uplift, the limestones, the modern corals and the relationships among them, and that he resolved to write a book on the geology of the voyage – there is an alternative spot. It is about 2 miles (3km) north-east, on the mainland coast, just below Flag Staff Hill. On his voyage home the *Beagle* called again briefly at St Jago (31 August to 4 September 1836). His remarks are brief, but echo the feelings that he had four and a half years before:

> As might be expected, I was not so much delighted with St Jago as during my first visit: but even this time I found its Natural History very interesting. It would indeed be strange if the first view of desert volcanic plains, (a kind of country so utterly different from anything in England) & the first sensations of an ardent climate, did not excite the most vivid impressions in the mind of every one, who takes pleasure in beholding the face of nature … .
>
> I confess, I feel some good will to the Island: I should be ungrateful if it was otherwise; for I shall never forget the delight of first standing in a certain lava cavern & looking at the swell of the Atlantic lashing the rugged shore.

It has been pointed out (e.g. in an article by Paul Pearson in *Four Centuries of Geological Travel*, Geological Society, London, 2007) that the last line of this description equates more closely to the Flag Staff Hill site than to any point on Quail Island (which is more sheltered), and thus is most likely to be the point where Darwin resolved to write his book, and where his scientific career could truly be said to have begun.

The *Beagle* left the Cape Verdes on 8 September, arriving off St Paul's Rocks, the tiny groups of islets almost on the Equator, a week later (see Chapter 6). Darwin had seen huge flocks of seabirds soaring above the islands, and noticed the brilliant white appearance of the bird droppings on the rocks. The boats had difficulty in landing because of the heavy swell, but when they managed to gain the shore they were surrounded on all sides by birds 'so unaccustomed to men that they would not move'.

Although Darwin was on land at St Paul's Rocks for a very few hours, his scientific observations were remarkable. There were, according to Darwin, only two sorts of birds – boobies and noddies. The boobies are a species of gannet, probably brown boobies (*Sula leucogaster*); the noddies are terns. Two rather similar species apparently breed on St Paul's: the common or brown noddy (*Anous stolidus*) and the white-capped noddy (*A. minutus*).

He noted in his diary that 'these with a few insects were the only organized beings that inhabited this desolate spot'. He obviously made a much more detailed study of the life-forms of the island than these superficial notes imply. He expands them in the *Voyage of the Beagle*, written shortly after the end of the voyage, into what amounts to an almost complete inventory of the island's biota. Like many scientists since, he perhaps found that the inherent simplicity of a very small island's ecosystem aided study, and allowed relationships to emerge that in a more complex community would be more difficult to discern. Here is his summary from the *Voyage of the Beagle*:

> The booby lays her eggs on the bare rock: but the tern makes a very simple nest with the seaweed. By the side of many of these nests a small flying fish was placed, which I suppose had been brought by the male bird for its partner.* It was amusing to watch how quickly a large and active crab (Graspus), which inhabits the crevices of the rock, stole the fish from the side of the nest, as soon as we had disturbed the parent birds. ... Not a single plant, not even a lichen, grows on the islet; yet it is inhabited by several insects and spiders. The following list completes, I believe the terrestrial fauna: a fly (Olfersia) living on the booby, and a tick which must have come here as a parasite; a small brown moth, belonging to a genus that feeds on feathers: a beetle (Quedius) and a woodlouse from beneath the dung; and lastly numerous spiders, which I suppose prey on these small attendants and scavengers of the waterfowl. ... The smallest rock in the tropical seas, by giving a foundation for the growth of innumerable kinds of seaweed and compound animals, supports likewise a large number of fish ... [including] sharks ...

(*In *Zoology of the Voyage of the Beagle, Part 3, Birds*, 1841, Darwin adds 'to feed on during the labour of incubation'.)

The fly specimens (two females) still exist and have been identified as *Olfersia aenescens*. The beetle specimen has been lost, but may have been the widespread *Quedius mesomelinus* or *Philonthus cliens*; the latter has been found subsequently at St Paul's. The moth was probably *Erechthias darwini*, which, it has been suggested, feeds on the dry seaweed of nesting material rather than feathers. An expedition to St Paul's in 1979 found a very similar range of organisms to what Darwin had recorded 150 years earlier.

It must be remembered that Darwin wrote the integrated account above years after his visit, but it is remarkable for its ecological awareness. The subject of ecology, with the concepts of ecological niches, food chains and food webs lay far in the future. Yet these few lines, written in about 1838, based on his notes and recollections of six years before, indicate an awareness of the unity of the ecosystem, of food relationships, and the links between the terrestrial and marine environment. It would be entirely possible to construct a food-web diagram from Darwin's observations. The account is of interest in other ways too: he is ahead of his time in mentioning aspects of the *behaviour* of organisms – the bringing of food for the mate; the scavenging of the crabs in the absence of adult birds. Quite trivial observations in themselves, but they were the precursors of ideas that were later of great importance in Darwin's work. (Darwin also wrote an extremely detailed account of the behaviour of an octopus he caught at St Jago.)

Darwin was not a 'finished' naturalist (as his friend and mentor John Henslow had put it) on going aboard the *Beagle*. He had sat through a few boring lectures in geology in Edinburgh; in the early summer of 1831 he had had a little instruction from Henslow, undertaken a few rather cursory excursions of the area around Shrewsbury ('I coloured a map') and then acted as trainee field assistant to Adam Sedgwick on a fortnight's excursion in North Wales. The geology of his first island was 'striking, yet simple': the horizontals of very gently dipping rocks were well exposed in cliffs and valley sides. There was little covering of vegetation (see Fig. 12). All in all it was the ideal environment for the young geologist to cut his teeth, to learn to see in three dimensions and to 'make out the geology of a district', prior to the complexities of South America, particularly the Andes, or even the much

13. Steeply folded rocks, East Falkland. *Photo by author*

more complex sets of steeply folded rocks of the Falklands (Fig. 13).

The dull lectures, Henslow's encouragement, some independent immature scratchings in the Welsh Borderland, Sedgwick's field training, St Jago, South America – the order could not have been better to ensure his logical development in training. Yet it was unplanned: it just happened that way.

It is almost as though Charles realized this. On leaving St Jago for the first time he wrote:

> Tomorrow we certainly sail. And I am glad of it, for I am impatient to see tropical vegetation in greater luxuriance than it can be seen here. Upon the whole the time has been the proper length & has flown away very pleasantly. (*Diary* entry 6 September 1832; possibly an error for 7th)

The 'proper length': it is as though he understood that he needed the time to get his eye in and to assimilate and put into practice what he had learnt on the 'striking yet simple geology'.

The open landscape of the tablelands of St Jago with their very arid climate appeared 'sterile'; there were relatively few species of plants and animals. The natural history of the tiny, isolated archipelago of St Paul's was even simpler (the biodiversity was very low, in modern parlance). Darwin was able to study them, and come to grips with the relationships they presented without difficulty, after 'walking with Henslow' in the fields of Cambridgeshire, and perhaps being trained in observation during his abortive period as a medical student. After the elegant simplicity of St Jago and St Paul's he was keen to sample the tropical luxuriance of a continental tropical environment.

It did not disappoint. On his first evening at Bahia in Brazil he conveyed the complexity of tropical environments well:

> The delight of experiences sometimes bewilders the mind; if the eye attempts to follow the flight of the gaudy butterfly it is arrested by some strange tree or fruit; if watching an insect one forgets it in the stranger flower it is crawling over … The mind is a chaos of delight. (*Diary*, 28 February 1832)

And the next day (Leap Year Day), after wandering alone in the Brazilian tropical rainforest:

The day has passed delightfully: delight is however a weak term for such transports of pleasure ... amongst the multitude it is hard to say what set of objects is the most striking; the general luxuriance of the vegetation bears the victory, the elegance of the grasses, the glossy green of the foliage, all tend to this end. A most paradoxical mixture of sound & silence pervades the shady part of the wood: the noise is so loud that in the evening it can be heard in a vessel anchored several hundred yards from the shore: yet within the recesses of the forest a universal stillness appears to reign.

The words 'bewilders', 'chaos' and 'paradoxical' clearly show that he appreciated the complexity of the plant and animal communities before him, even if he did not understand it fully.

Just as it was Darwin's luck to see the unfolded, relatively recent rocks of St Jago before the tight folds of the Andes or the complex igneous intrusions of Tasmania, so it was a steady development from casual beetle hunting in Wales and East Anglia with his cousin William Darwin Fox, to the unravelling of the simple food-relationships of St Paul's to astonishment at the complexity of tropical ecosystems.

And so it continued. There are innumerable instances during the *Beagle* voyage, where Charles Darwin was not only fortunate in the places that he visited, but fortunate in having visited them in a particular order.

One instance of this was the development of his 'coral atoll theory', his (successful) attempt to explain the circular nature of coral atolls, and to place them in a sequence:

Fringing reefs → barrier reefs → atolls

In a letter dated 29 April 1836, to his sister Caroline, he said: 'The subject of Coral formation, has for the past half year been a point of particular interest to me.' This would take the date of his first deliberations on the subject of coral to late October 1835, when he was in the Galapagos, however, just before he was on the coast of South America, where, in several places, he had noted evidence of elevation of the land in the form of beach deposits with marine shells far above modern shorelines. In his *Autobiography*, written many years later, he stated that: 'the whole theory [of coral reef formation] was thought out on the west coast of S America before I had seen a coral reef.' Moreover, in one of his 'little note books', there are entries probably written in Chile in 1835, which include the following fragmentary speculations:

> [I]n Pacific a Coral bed forming as land sunk would abound with those genera which live near the surface (mixed with those of deep water) ...
>
> Is there a large proportion of those coralls which live only near the surface. – If so we must believe the land sinking.
>
> The Test of depression in strata is where great thickness has shallow coralls growing in situ: this could only happen where bottom of the ocean was subsiding.

Finally there is a letter dated 25 June 1835, from R. E. Alison, who had assisted Darwin with some of his studies in Chile, saying how much he was looking forward to Darwin's reports on the Pacific islands for 'it will be curious if you find sinking of land there, & rising here ...' Darwin, in the Falklands, in Chiloé and several times on the mainland of South America had looked for, and sometimes felt he had found, evidence of changing levels of land and sea, and it seems that even before he had seen a coral island, he was speculating on the possibility of subsidence of the Pacific islands, in some way compensating for a rise in the level of South America.

On 13 November 1835 the ship was passing through the main mass of the 'Low or Dangerous' Archipelago, and Darwin noted that at daylight, and again at noon, they had recorded two islands that were not on the charts. (FitzRoy, probably after discussing the matter with people in Tahiti, refers to the 'native names' of Tairo and Cavahi; Taiaro and Kauehi appear on modern maps. The Captain continues that the ship passed 'between the Elizabeth and Wittgenstein [or Faarava] groups'. Modern maps include Fakarava.)

Despite his professed hatred of ships and the sea, and frequent seasickness, Darwin seems to have brought himself to climb to the masthead to view the islands. His description is quite detailed:

> ... a long and brilliantly white beach is capped by a low bright line of green vegetation. This stripe on both hands, rapidly appears to narrow & sinks beneath the horizon. The width of dry land is very trifling; from the Mast-head it was possible

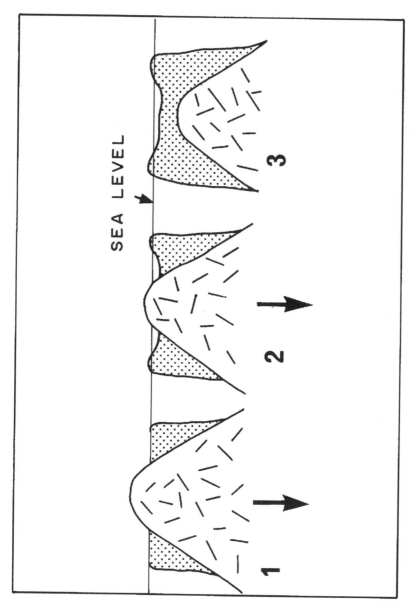

14. Formation of coral atolls. With the submergence of an island, or a rise in sea level, a fringing reef becomes a barrier reef and eventually an atoll.

to see at Noon Island across the smooth lagoon to the opposite side. This great lake of water was about 10 miles wide. (*Diary*, 13 November 1835)

This sighting strengthened Darwin's fascination with coral atolls, the fascination that ultimately resulted in the publication of Volume 1 of the *Geology of the Voyage: the Structure and Distribution of Coral Reefs* and which represented one of his first flirtations with the notion of gradualism.

He took a particular interest in the island of Eimeo (now called Moorea) which he viewed from a point in Tahiti above Point Venus, with its jagged rocky interior, surrounding lagoon, and barrier of coral beyond.

> From this point, there was a good view of the distant island of Eimeo ... On the lofty & broken pinnacles white massive clouds were piled, which formed an island in the blue sky, as Eimeo itself in the blue ocean. The island is completely circled by a reef, with the exception of a small gateway. At this distance a narrow but well defined line of brilliant white, where the waves first encountered the wall of coral, was alone visible. Within this line was included the smooth glassy water of the lagoon, out of which the mountains rose abruptly. The effect was very pleasing & might aptly be compared to a framed engraving, where the frame represents the breakers, the marginal paper the lagoon, & the drawing the Island itself. (*Diary*, 17 November 1835)

Darwin also made extensive observations of the reefs around Tahiti, probably using both a boat and 'jumping pole'. He was trying to find confirmation in the field of a theory he had already constructed in his mind.

Among Darwin's *Beagle* Geological Notes in the Cambridge University Library is a 23-page manuscript, apparently rather hastily written in Darwin's hand. Entitled 'Coral Islands', it is likely that it was written on board ship during the crossing from Tahiti to New Zealand, between 3 and 21 December 1835. It is in this document that we see Darwin's first coherent expression of his theory that fringing reefs (in which coral reefs are closely attached to the shore), barrier reefs (where there is a peripheral moat-like lagoon) and true atolls (Darwin sometimes called these 'lagoon islands', circular or horseshoe-shaped groups of islets with a central lagoon) are members of a series, one form developing into another as the result of subsidence. Indeed

15. Point Venus: one of the *Beagle* anchorage points in Tahiti. Darwin undertook extensive fieldwork near here, developing his 'Theory of Coral Reefs', his first experimentation with the notion of gradualism – Gradual Change. *Photo by author*

this represents Darwin's first real embrace of the notion of gradualism in his own work. This idea of long-continued very gradual change being the main factor in sculpting the earth's surface he had partly acquired from his reading of Lyell's *Principles of Geology*, which emphasized uniformitarianism, rather than catastrophism. In the 'Coral Islands' manuscript Charles Darwin briefly repeats his description of Eimeo:

> The mountains rise out of a glassy lake, which is separated on all sides, by a narrow defined line of breakers, from the open sea.– Remove the central group of mountains, & there remains a Lagoon Isd.– I ground this opinion from the following facts.– There is a general similarity in the two cases in the form & size of their reefs; their structure appears identical, we have scarcely fathomable water in each case, at a very short distance on the outer margin; within is a shallow basin more or less filled

16. Coral coast, West Island, Cocos (Keeling) Islands, Indian Ocean. Darwin found confirmation of his 'Theory of Coral Reefs' during the week that he spent at this tiny archipelago. *Photo by author*

17. Coral rock, West Island, Cocos (Keeling) Islands, Indian Ocean. *Photo by author*

by knolls of growing coral or converted into dry land.– In the Lagoon Isds there are some which do not deserve this title for they consist solely of a circular reef of which scarcely a point projects above water; while others have a more or less complete, but narrow ring of land. ('Coral Islands', DAR 40/5. The document is transcribed by D. R. Stoddart in *Atoll Research Bulletin*, 88, 1962.)

The small-scale features of reefs are also closely described in the document; from his fieldwork in Tahiti, he recalls how the outer 'mound' or 'breakwater' of living coral slopes inwards, towards the smooth waters of the lagoon.

> The sea, breaking violently on the outer margin, continuously pumps over in sheets the water of its waves. – Hence the surface is worn smooth & gently declines toward the lagoon. ('Coral Islands')

Elsewhere in the account he noted that the coral growth was most rapid and prolific on the outer edge of the reef; this was the home of certain specific types of coral. He accurately suggested that this might be due either to 'the motion of the water or the quantity of insolved air'.

He summarizes:

> [I]n certain parts of the Pacifick, a series of subsidences have taken place; of which no one exceeded in depth the number of ft at which ... polypi will flourish: & [where] the successive steps were sufficiently long to allow their growth. ('Coral Islands')

He concluded, once again, by speculating that the rise in the level of South America was compensated for by depression in the Pacific.

Having had vague inklings in South America, glimpsed atolls from afar from the masthead, then having explored both the micro- and the macro-features of coral reefs in Tahiti, he penned his draft theory. After leaving Australia the *Beagle* visited (in April 1836) the Cocos (Keeling) Islands in the Indian Ocean. In the course of a week's sojourn (it was the first time he had actually set foot on an atoll), Darwin was able to visit several islands of the little archipelago, and confirm to his own satisfaction that his theory was broadly correct. Among other studies, he was able to establish by sounding from the vessel offshore that the seabed fell away very sharply from the island, giving support to the idea that the coral atoll was atop a submarine mountain peak.

This little archipelago provided a case-study chapter in his book on Coral Islands (Volume 1 of the *Geology of the Voyage of the Beagle*). He wrote, on leaving, 'I was glad that we visited these islands': a major understatement, for he was able to put the finishing touches to his theory, which was his first use of the gradualist, or uniformitarian notion, that when a simple process (in this case subsidence) is continued for long periods of time, great changes in form and structure can be effected.

Nor was this the end of it. Just over two weeks after departing from Cocos, the *Beagle* called at Mauritius, where further gaps could be filled. Here was another island with fringing reefs, but where evidence of *uplift* could be seen locally for masses of coral rock could be seen above the present sea level.

From building the idea in South America, seeing evidence for uplift and reading Lyell's book, the evidence came tumbling in, in the right order ('Dangerous Archipelago' – Tahiti – Cocos – Mauritius) and it seems at a rate that Darwin could accommodate. The sea voyage between Tahiti and New Zealand (or perhaps New Zealand to Australia) provided the opportunity for the leisurely sifting of observations, and clarification of ideas.

It would be too much to say that Darwin became a gradualist because he visited certain islands in a particular order. But in the course of a little over a year the coral atoll hypothesis took form, as each island and group of islands provided a different assemblage of environments and opportunities.

The increasing biological and geological complexity of the Atlantic islands, following so soon after his training by Henslow and Sedgwick in East Anglia and North Wales, provided a proving ground prior to Brazil's tropical forests, the Andes and the islands of South America (the Falklands, Tierra del Fuego and Chiloé). Those of the Pacific and Indian Oceans allowed ideas anent to those of evolutionary change to develop.

8

Darwin's Women

Darwin's early life was dominated by women. We have noted that he had four sisters, ranging in age from 11 years his senior to 15 months his junior (see Chapter 3). But there was another dimension: for several generations the Darwins were close to the Wedgwood family. Robert Darwin and Josiah Wedgwood II, the second generation of the pottery manufacturing dynasty, had been good friends, and the friendship continued into the generation beyond. Josiah Wedgwood II and Elizabeth (née Allen) had nine children – five girls and four boys. One of the girls died in infancy, a decade before Charles came onto the scene. The others were Elizabeth (born 1793), Charlotte (1797), Frances or Fanny (1806) and Emma (1808). At the time with which we are concerned the family lived at Maer, just over the border in Staffordshire some 30 miles (50km) north-east of Shrewsbury, where they owned a large Elizabethan house, on a substantial estate with a lake and some woodland. The young Charles Darwin used to regularly ride over to Maer, particularly for the partridge shooting. The young Darwins and Wedgwoods all seem to have enjoyed each other's company; they put on plays together and held musical evenings. There was probably a certain amount of flirtation. At any event Caroline Darwin married Josiah Wedgwood III (the eldest male Wedgwood) in 1837. At one stage there was a suggestion of a friendship between Charles and Fanny.

Charles Darwin certainly enjoyed female company, and was impressed by feminine charms. In about September 1829 he attended a concert in Birmingham, and writing to another cousin, William Darwin Fox, at

Osmaston, he described it as 'the most glorious thing I ever experienced'. Of the soloist, one of the great contraltos of her day, Maria Felicia Garcia (she sang under the name of first husband, Malibran), he wrote: 'words cannot praise her enough, she is quite the most charming person I ever saw.'

But the crush on the beautiful singer was a passing one, and the friendship with Fanny Wedgwood seems to have had little depth, although his sister Catherine certainly thought the relationship might have possibilities some time later when she taunted him with her opinion that she would make an excellent wife!

There was another Fanny, in whom he was far more interested during the summers of the late 1820s. William Mostyn Owen had formerly served as an officer in the Royal Dragoons, and was described as a 'peppery and despotic squire of the old school'. But he had assets. He had a large, well-wooded estate full of game at Woodhouse, not too far distant from either Maer or Shrewsbury. And he had daughters – Sarah and Fanny – about whom Charles had heard quite a lot, after they had had singing lessons with some of the Darwin sisters at The Mount. 'They are very much to be admired', his younger sister and former playmate Catherine commented. She preferred Fanny: 'there is something ... engaging and delightful about her.'

And so it proved. Sarah was too old for him, five years his senior, although the two carried on a sporadic correspondence, at one stage, and she sent him a cravat pin before he embarked on the *Beagle*. He told his cousin William Fox that both the Owen sisters were 'idols of my adoration'. But Fanny – Fanny Mostyn Owen – had an extra something. She was dark-haired, bright-eyed, petite, and she had such spirit! She enjoyed playing billiards with the boys, and Charles Darwin and she often went riding in the woodlands at Woodhouse. There is an incident, tantalizingly referred to obliquely in correspondence, which may have occurred in the early summer of 1827 (when Charles was 18), when they were together in the sunshine in the strawberry beds at Woodhouse gorging themselves on the fruit. This doesn't seem to have been a secretive tryst, and must have been witnessed by both Susan Darwin and Caroline Owen, the next youngest sister, for both referred to it affectionately in correspondence years later.

Another incident illustrates the spirit of this remarkable young woman. She insisted on firing a gun, under Darwin's tutelage. Partly for reasons of decorum, but also because of the powerful kick on firing, women seldom shot. One can see the toss of the head and flick of the hair as she insisted that her boyfriend help her. Darwin long remembered 'how charming she looked when she insisted on firing'. The recoil is said to have made her 'black and blue' yet she 'gave no sign' of discomfort. The young sportsman was clearly passionately in love with her. At one stage Darwin wrote of his 'dearest Fanny' and in a letter to his cousin William Fox described her as the 'prettiest, plumpest [in certain parts of her body, presumably], [most] charming personage that Shropshire possesses'. They exchanged small gifts and conducted a protracted correspondence over several years, referring to each other as Postillion (possibly an allusion to the blue jacket Charles wore, something similar to a groom's livery, perhaps) and Housemaid (the young woman who didn't like remaining at home? Or who prided herself on her terrible handwriting?). Many of Fanny's letters are the scatterbrained effusions of a young woman about parties and balls and the 'shootables', the name her sister gave to eligible young bachelors, there encountered. These were no doubt intended to fan a little flame of envy in the mind of the young Darwin. Possibly there is some sexual innuendo intended in the frequent references to the postillion and the housemaid, for these were the servants in large houses who were sometimes involved in unauthorized liaisons with the gentry families. Some have seen significance in the frequent requests at the end of Fanny's letters to Charles to 'burn this'. But there is absolutely no evidence that the relationship was ever more than an adolescent, if extremely passionate, crush.

Indeed, it may be that Charles's feelings were the stronger. The sometimes rather serious young man may have been bowled over by the vivacious charm, good looks and high spirits of a girl who endured painting lessons for the sake of her father. Yet when he communicated with her elder sister Sarah, after leaving Edinburgh, and theological study at Cambridge and a life in a country parsonage were in prospect, the younger sister wrote back to him:

18. Letter from Darwin, to his cousin William Fox, in which he describes his girlfriend Fanny Owen: '[A]s all the world knows [she] is the prettiest, plumpest [most] charming personage that Shropshire possesses.' *By kind permission of the Master and Fellows of Christ's College, Cambridge*

I was very much surprised to hear from Sarah that you have decided to become a DD [Doctor of Divinity] instead of an MD. You never let me into the secret.

And later:

I cannot & will not play second fiddle.

And one winter after he had gone up to Cambridge:

Why did you not come home this Xmas? ... I fully expected to have seen you – but I suppose some dear little Beetles in Cambridge or London kept you away.

Fanny may not have been as open and ingenuous as some of her dashed-off scrawls suggest. She seems to have had, at least for a while, some sort of understanding with a John Hill, a clergyman, brother of the local Tory MP, and scion of a notable local family. In late summer of 1830 Charles was summoned to Woodhouse, not just to 'slay partridges' but for a frank talk with Squire Owen. Fanny became engaged to the Reverend John Hill, often known as 'The Hill'. But the marriage did not take place: the sources vary as to the precise nature of the estrangement. There are hints in some of Susan's letters that he broke it off. On the other hand some sources imply that Fanny's mother had a hand in things. In March 1832 she married Myddleton Biddulph, a wealthy, rakish, aspiring politician, he perhaps catching her on the rebound. He had been a heavy gambler. The wedding had been sumptuous, and a few months later she had been by his side canvassing for his election as MP for Denbigh. They lived very grandly at Chirk Castle. When Charles received letters from his sisters describing the nuptials he is said to have cried.

There were others. He seems briefly to have cast an eye on his cousin, the 'incomparable' Charlotte Wedgwood, even though she was 12 years older than himself. One letter from 'la belle Fanny' teased him about some other girl who was alleged to be his latest 'lovee'.

Darwin was certainly happy in the company of attractive women, and seems to have flirted mildly with señoritas in South America, and he certainly enjoyed the companionship of some 'very nice looking young ladies' at a luncheon party at Vineyard, the Macarthur family property at Parramatta, New South Wales, in January 1836. They included the elder four of Maria and Hanibal Macarthur's six daughters: Elizabeth, who was then aged 20, Annie, who was 19, Catherine, 17, and Mary, 14. Charles was not the only one to be attracted to this bevy of young women: two of his shipmates eventually married Macarthur daughters (John Wickam married Annie in 1842, and Philip King [junior] married Elizabeth in 1843). It has been suggested on rather flimsy evidence that shortly after his return from the *Beagle* voyage, he had some interest in a Catherine Horner, daughter of a politically aware geologist friend of Charles Lyell. But none compared with his passionate, long-lasting fondness for Fanny. There are signs in the writings of one of his daughters, Henrietta, that he remembered her with great affection for the rest of his life. He sent her flowers shortly after returning from the *Beagle*; in her third pregnancy, languishing in her Welsh castle, she was overcome.

There is one final piece of coincidence we may note. After the breaking of her engagement with 'The Hill', Fanny Owen was despatched to stay with friends in the West of England. When Charles was down at Devonport with Captain FitzRoy having a preliminary inspection of the *Beagle* in September 1831, she was 'doing her penance' after the break-up, at Exeter just 50 miles away. Indeed they both may have been in Plymouth the same day: they may have been within a few hundred yards of one another, but never met. There was another exchange of letters just before his sailing. Fanny wrote him a very long letter and sent him a 'leetle purse' and wrote that she longed to see him again, and on his return she would be:

> … in status quo at the Forest [their name for Woodhouse], only grown old and sedate … The many happy hours we have had together from the time we were Housemaid and Postillion … are not to be forgotten … & would that there was not to be an end of them!!. I don't know what we shall do at the forest without you. (Exclamation marks in original; Fanny Owen to Charles Darwin, postmarked Exeter, 6 October 1831)

This sounds like a *crie de coeur*. But it was too late. A further letter was received by Charles while he was in Brazil, just before she married Biddulph, and strikes a similar note:

> My fate is indeed decided, the die is cast – and my dear Charles I feel quite certain I have not a friend in the world more sincerely [interested] in my welfare than you are ... I do think mine is a happy end, I have no misgivings about it ... I would give a great deal to see you again & have one more merry chat, whilst I am still Fanny Owen, but alas that cannot be ... [W]hen you do return to the little Parsonage and want the little wife! Pray give me the commission to look out for her. [Y]ou will always find me the same sincere friend I have always been ever since we were Housemaid and Postillion together. ... Now adieu and Heaven bless you my very dear Charles.

There was a good deal more. It is almost that she doth protest too much. It was certainly a strangely effusive letter for a girl to send to a former boyfriend on the eve of her wedding.

'A first love is a special love.' The frequent meetings, the rides in the forests, the steadying of her gun when he was teaching her to shoot, the unaffected manner in which the courtship was remembered by other members of the families, the fact that the 'Housemaid–Postilion' fantasy continued for years, seem to vouch for the truth of this saying. The fact that Fanny asked Charles to 'burn this' at the end of almost every letter (and the fact that he didn't, but kept them carefully) also tells of a strong emotional link. Alas, no letter from Charles to Fanny has been found (perhaps they were all destroyed at the time of her first or second engagement or her marriage, to prevent damage to her reputation).

Over four and a half years had passed since Darwin had read Fanny's last emotional letter, received while he was in South America. On the 'dreadfully stormy' night of 2 October 1836, HMS *Beagle* anchored at Falmouth, Cornwall, in the extreme south-west of England. 'That same night', he wrote on the final page of his diary, 'I started by the Mail for Shrewsbury.' All the next day and the day after, he was travelling, the coaches stopping from time to time at inns for the refreshment of passengers and to change horses. He must have had to change coaches once or twice. On he went, the horses no doubt kicking up damp autumn leaves as they galloped along.

Charles was impatient to be home, but probably a little anxious at what he might find there after his five years away. He arrived in the 'good old town of Shrewsbury' late at night on 4 October. Not wishing to disturb his family, he spent the night at an inn, walking in through the front door of The Mount early the following morning.

One can imagine the scene: the hugs, the kisses, the beaming sisterhood, the tears, the spluttering out of incomplete tales; the great figure of Dr Robert smiling benignly, a little in the background. The prodigal son had returned and the fatted calf was about to be slain. Certainly the household had a few drinks: Darwin wrote to his former Captain: 'Two or three of our labourers ... set to work, and got excessively drunk in honour of the arrival of Master Charles' (Charles Darwin to Robert FitzRoy, 6 October 1836).

A few hours after his arrival at The Mount, Charles was renewing links with the Wedgwood clan at Maer, writing to Uncle Jos, who had supported his proposal to go aboard the *Beagle*:

> My head is quite confused with so much delight, but I cannot allow my sisters to tell you first how happy I am to see all my dear friends again ... I am most anxious once again to see Maer and all its inhabitants, so that in the course of the next two or three weeks, I hope in person to thank you, as being my First Lord of the Admiralty. (5 October 1836)

And he was as good as his word. In the latter part of October Emma Wedgwood significantly wrote: 'We are getting impatient for Charles's arrival.' She obviously wanted to make an impression, for she had been reading a book on South America, called *Rapid Journeys across the Pampas* (by Sir Francis Head). And immediately after his visit she reported: 'We enjoyed Charles's visit uncommonly.' It seems as though a little warmth was already developing, for Charles gave her some 'feather flowers' (some sort of hair or hat decoration, perhaps?), which were 'much admired' during a round of social events in Edinburgh, where Emma was staying for a while early in 1837.

Charles, meanwhile, was working as he had never worked before: sorting his specimens and notes, and making scientific contacts with those who were to receive his specimens in order to describe and classify them, attending meetings of the Geological Society, and commencing his writing programme. He stayed with his brother Erasmus in London, then with the Henslows in Cambridge, and then nearby in rented accommodation in Fitzwilliam Street, Cambridge. Then back to 'odious, smokey' London. The odium and the pollution had to be endured so that he could be close to the leading men of science with whom he had to converse. At Charles Lyell's instigation he attended some of the brilliant parties of Charles Babbage, the mathematician and pioneer in the field of computers. He wrote to his sister Caroline, early in 1837, that he had been told that attending these soirées was the best way of meeting influential people in literary London and that there was 'a good mixture of pretty women' at such gatherings. And as we have seen, Darwin liked pretty women! In February 1838, he somewhat reluctantly accepted the position of secretary of the Geological Society. At this time too, he was developing his theories on the transmutability of species in his series of little notebooks.

On several occasions during 1837 and 1838, Darwin managed to tear himself away from his work to visit Maer and Shrewsbury. Perhaps his father and sisters were the excuse, and Emma was the reason. In the summer of 1838 they went to the village fête together. In August he wrote a very cheerful letter to her:

> This Marlborough St. is a forlorn place – we have no ducks here, much less any geese, & as for that sentimental fat goose we ate over the Library fire, – the like of it seldom turns up. I feel … spiteful joy at hearing you have had no other geese. (Charles Darwin to Emma Wedgwood, 7 August 1838)

This needs a bit of decoding. There were probably duck on the lake at Maer. Darwin may have even shot at some of them in his time. The 'goose' was the long and memorable conversation they had in the library at Maer earlier in the summer. It was 'sentimental' and 'fat' – concerned with personal relationships and thus very important, perhaps. Later in the letter he writes, tantalizingly: 'so see me you will … [and] we will have another goose.' He ends: 'Believe me dear Emma, yours most sincerely Chas. Darwin'. And then

19. Emma Darwin as a young woman. Portrait by George Raymond, from the late 1830s.

perhaps not wanting to blow it by overstepping the mark, he crossed out 'dear'!

He went back to London, working hard on his books and scientific papers, but a part of his mind was elsewhere. In the rough diary he kept at this time he jotted 'November 9th Started for Maer'. Two days later occurs the note 'Sunday. The day of days.' He went to Shrewsbury the next day (12th), presumably to give his father and his sisters the news that he had proposed to Emma and she had accepted. He returned to Maer on 17 November as Emma's fiancé, and then hurried back to London.

Charles's sisters wholeheartedly approved: they had expected it, although they were slightly surprised by the suddenness of developments. Dr D wrote to Josiah Wedgwood saying, 'Emma having consented to marry Charles gives me as much pleasure as Jos [Josiah junior] having married Caroline, and I cannot say more.' Uncle Jos replied: 'If I could have given such a wife to Charles without parting with a daughter there would have been no drawback in my entire satisfaction in bestowing Emma upon him.' He settled £5,000 on her and granted her an allowance of £400 a year.

Emma was clearly smitten. To a friend she penned the following:

He is the most open, transparent man I ever saw, and every word expresses his real thoughts. He is particularly affectionate and very nice to his father and sisters, and perfectly sweet tempered, and possesses some minor qualities that add particularly to one's happiness, such as not being fastidious [five years of living in the cramped quarters of the *Beagle* and of outback travel would have seen to that], and being humane to animals.

She was under no illusions: she understood the programme of scientific work that lay ahead. Although he 'stands concerts very well', he had a 'great dislike' of the theatre.

Perhaps, despite the 'geese' they had had, Charles felt he might have been a little undemonstrative, for he wrote back soon after leaving her after the acceptance:

[T]here never was anybody so *lucky* as I have been, or so good as you. – Indeed I can assure you, many times since leaving Maer, I have thought how little I expressed how much I owe to you ... I vow to try to make myself good enough to somewhat deserve you.

Italics added, although on this occasion at least Darwin understood his good fortune, or at least understood the importance of 'making his own luck'!

It could have been otherwise. Some time in 1837 or 1838 Charles took up a piece of paper and prepared what now might be called a crude cost–benefit analysis, comparing the advantages of marriage as against a bachelor existence. (In fact there are two such documents, probably compiled at about the same time.) Peter Brent, in his 1981 biography of Darwin, expressed the view that this was in April 1838, and links the analysis to his thoughts about Catherine Horner (see above, page 92) as a possible bride. In the document itself, however, there is absolutely no indication that he was thinking about anyone in particular. Two columns are headed 'Marry' and 'Not Marry', and the advantages and disadvantages of marriage and the bachelor life are mercilessly listed. Among the advantages for not marrying were the possibility of further travel: to Europe, to the USA, to Mexico perhaps?, 'not [being] forced to visit relatives', not having the expense and anxiety of children, and being able to afford to spend more on books.

In the 'Marry' tabulation is to be found the following:

Children – (if it please God) – constant companion, (friend in old age) who will feel interested in one, object to be beloved and played with – better than a dog anyhow – Home, and someone to take care of the house – Charms of music and female chit-chat. These things are good for one's health. Forced to visit and receive relations *but terrible loss of time.*

But at the foot are the words 'Marry – Marry – Marry'. And also the little jotting 'keep a good look out' which tends to suggest that there was indeed no particular individual in view when this analysis was made!

Pleased as Dr Darwin was at the engagement, and the prospect of further developing the links between the two families, he was wont to give advice, and at the time of the engagement, and before, and after, he gave a good deal to Charles. Such was Robert Darwin's influence on his younger son that Charles listened to most of it. Dr Darwin had much to say about housing, and also discussed the medical risks involved in repeated marriages between cousins. He also advised Charles not to discuss the nature of any religious doubts he might have with his spouse: this was a piece of advice that Charles did NOT accept.

Darwin travelled back and forth between London, Maer and Shrewsbury several times between November 1838 and late January 1839, when he and Emma were married. Emma would have liked a spring wedding, but Charles, having decided on a course of action, wanted to get on with the matter at hand.

Emma was 30, and some might have said slightly old to be embarking on the business of childbearing for the first time. But she was, as biographer Peter Brent has put it, 'tall of brow, wide of jaw, with a well-shaped, witty mouth, intelligent eyes set far apart and the short, strong Wedgwood nose'. She was musical, quite well read, knew several languages, and … a wealthy woman.

They were married at Maer Church on 29 January 1839 by the Rev Allan Wedgwood. One guest said the wedding was like one of those in Jane Austen's novels. Darwin was no doubt elated at having just been elected a Fellow of the Royal Society (Britain's highest scientific honour) five days before. Now there's Darwin's luck!

There has been speculation as to the extent, or otherwise, of Darwin's sexual experience at the time of his marriage to Emma. There is no evidence either way. During, and immediately before, the *Beagle* voyage, he was contemplating a career as a Church of England priest, and promiscuity would surely be incompatible with this aspiration. The ports of South America were dens of prostitution and very probably, despite Captain FitzRoy's puritanical views, some of the crew (both lower deck and 'gun room') indulged. Earlier he and Erasmus must have been exposed to prostitution in Edinburgh, and the Barnwell district of Cambridge was noted for its young women, some of whom, from poor labouring families in the Fens, flocked to Cambridge to provide for the needs of some wealthy young gentlemen! Such men ran the risk of catching the 'Barnwell ague'. In residence about a decade later than Darwin's time in Cambridge, the shiftless undergraduate who later became the Reverend Charles Kingsley – novelist, polymath, political activist, canon of Chester and Westminster, and keen supporter of evolutionary ideas – admitted, guiltily, that he had been with a prostitute while at university. (Both Professors Sedgwick and Henslow were University Proctors, and among their duties was to round up women thought to be soliciting in Cambridge and ensure their punishment.) Darwin certainly must have been exposed to temptation, but he wrote to Sarah Owen early in his Cambridge residence that 'he had not set eyes on a girl since leaving home'.

But probably, while they were engaged, Emma and Charles displayed their affection for each other in the way that young couples do. Darwin was amidst his earlier speculations on evolutionary change, and had read Malthus's *On Population*. James Moore and Adrian Desmond in their biography *Darwin* (1991) have pointed out that a fortnight after his engagement, probably thinking about his own feelings while he was with Emma, and the pleasures of kissing her, he wrote in one of his notebooks:

> November 27th. – Sexual desire makes saliva flow, yes certainly – curious association: I have seen Nina [a dog] licking her chops. – someone has described slovering teethless-jaws. As picture of disgusting lewd old man. Ones tendency to kiss, & almost bite, that which one sexually loves is probably connected with flow of saliva, & hence the action of mouth & jaws. – Lascivious women are described as biting: so do stallions always.

Blushing might also be sexual, he thought, as it increases when men and women interacted. Blushing, kissing, slobbering and other symptoms of sexual arousal could perhaps be traced back to humanity's animal ancestors. Maybe, he pondered, thinking about one's appearance 'drives blood to the surface exposed, face of man ... bosom in woman: like erection'.

The vicissitudes of the marriage are discussed elsewhere, but Emma supported her husband through his illnesses (real or imagined), coped with his foibles, bore his ten children, and made a home that was remembered with affection by her grandchildren some 60 years after her passing.

The relationship is perhaps best summarized by the following extract from Darwin's *Autobiography*, written toward the end of his life, for his family:

You all know well your Mother, and what a good Mother she has ever been to all of you. She has been my greatest blessing, and I can declare that in my whole life I have never heard her utter one word which I had rather have been unsaid. She has never failed in the kindest sympathy towards me, and has borne with the utmost patience my frequent complains from ill-health and discomfort. I do not believe she has ever missed an opportunity of doing a kind action to anyone near her. I marvel at my good fortune that she, so infinitely my superior in every single moral quality, consented to be my wife. She has been my wise adviser and cheerful comforter throughout life, which without her would have been during a very long period a miserable one from ill-health. She has earned the love and admiration of every soul near her.

Was it good luck or bad luck that Charles and Fanny missed each other that day in Plymouth in 1831? Was it a sad, heartstring-tugging 'might have been'? Bumping into one another in such circumstances might have changed everything. They might have held each other in their arms, and taken the meeting as Providence's signal. Darwin might have withdrawn from the *Beagle* voyage and they might have settled in a country rectory ...

But if he had, then the history of the world would have been very different. Lively, attractive, indeed 'sexy', she might have been. But her letters are full of gossip and tittle-tattle – little but horses, flirtations and marriages, as one biographer put it. She loved parties and balls, and, probably, fine clothes. Darwin hated dancing. He read scientific books, and also while he was a student, Shakespeare's plays and poetry. She liked trite 'juicy' novels and novellas. She seems to have been rather vain and a little selfish. She had a quick wit, but was rather shallow. She was extravagant. Had they married, Darwin could not have kept up with her social demands for long, and she would have found him, and his scientific friends, boring. Despite sadnesses Darwin went on to a contented life. Fanny's marriage does not seem to have been so happy: she had to endure an extremely bitter mother-in-law and a good deal of illness.

9

From London's 'Dirt, Noise, Vice and Misery' to an 'Extraordinarily Rural and Quiet Village'

After they were married in January 1839, Charles and Emma lived in London for several years, in a rather ugly rented terraced house in Upper Gower Street. It was decorated and furnished in a rather kitsch manner. Some of the walls were brilliant blue, and the curtains bright yellow. The colours reminded Charles of a South American species of bird (the blue-and-yellow macaw, *Ara ararauna*), and they called the place Macaw Cottage. There was a dead dog in the garden. But the neighbourhood was quiet, and they were close to the young University College, which might have its advantages, although the link with Dr Grant, who had been something of an inspiration in Edinburgh days, and who had a room at the college, had been broken. They no longer got on. And Regent's Park was quite close, for walks.

Although there was the happiness of their getting closer to one another, there were also misfortunes and worries. Two days into their marriage they had news that Sophie, the 6-week-old child of Charles's sister Caroline (married to Emma's brother), had died at the age of 6 weeks. Caroline was 38, Josiah 43. The child had been weak – 'a poor puny little delicate thing' – from the start. The fact that the first child of a first-cousin marriage had perished in this way must have preyed on the minds of Charles and Emma as they started their life together. And then there was 'the servant problem', often a source of trial to the inexperienced young gentlewoman. Syms Covington, who had been Darwin's servant, scientific assistant and amanuensis since *Beagle* days, left to go to Australia just days after their setting up house. Personal recommendations were sometimes useless: 'The cook

from Shrewsbury is a failure as she cannot cook, & has a drunken husband.'
A maid turned out to be 'vulgar'.

Friends and relatives varied in their degree of support. Darwin had opened
his secret notebooks, and was beginning to experiment with his ideas of
transmutation, as he called it. He tried out some of the ideas he was playing
with on his cousin Hensleigh Wedgwood: he thought them 'absurd'. Another
frustration was the length of time that it was taking Captain FitzRoy to
complete his account of the voyage: Darwin had finished his many months
earlier, and as the three sections – one by Captain King on the first (1826)
voyage, FitzRoy's account, and Darwin's condensation of his diary – were to
appear in a single volume, FitzRoy's dilatoriness was holding up the whole
enterprise.

There were other concerns. Emma was pregnant within a few months of
marriage, and was sickly during some of her pregnancy. Charles, perhaps
worried lest the fate of baby Sophie, should also befall their own firstborn,
was also unwell. He said that the pregnancy had 'knocked him up' almost
as much as Emma. He remained unwell for many weeks, and missed several
meetings of the Geological Society: as he, at this time, was the Society's
secretary, this was no trifle.

Parts of the country were very disturbed. Millions signed the Charter,
pleading for democratic rights for all men, that was presented to, and rejected
by, Parliament. There was rioting in Birmingham (where Darwin went for a
meeting of the British Association for the Advancement of Science), and in
November a somewhat ill-planned attempt at insurrection in South Wales.
The disturbances were put down ruthlessly. The ringleaders were arrested
and tried for various offences including treason and sedition. A number
were sentenced to death, but although some individuals died in prison in
no case was a death sentence carried out. Many were, however, eventually
transported to Australia. For many months the country seemed to be teeter-
ing on the verge of revolution.

Emma's worries were magnified by thoughts of where her husband's
speculations (about which she had known since before they were married)
were taking him religiously. She was honestly concerned for her beloved's

immortal soul. Yet another source of worry to Charles was his brother Erasmus's devotion to opium. At times he lived in his own hazy world 'with many groans'.

But there were bright spots. In the middle of the year 1839 Darwin's first book – the volume that eventually became *The Voyage of the Beagle* – was published. Some reviewers thought it was a mistake for the three sections to be published bound together, and a few months later it appeared on its own. There were dinner parties at which scientists and writers such as Charles Lyell, Hensleigh Wedgwood, Richard Owen and the Swiss botanist Augustin de Candolle mingled. Emma struggled to cope.

Four days after Christmas 1839 Emma gave birth to William Erasmus Darwin; Emma's sister Elizabeth was on hand to help. Charles's health remained very poor; yet doctors were unable to diagnose anything of substance. Darwin spent much of the summer of 1840 at Maer and Shrewsbury, and he claimed he was able to do very little work. However, Emma was soon pregnant again and Anne Elizabeth followed William into the world on 2 March 1841. William was described as 'delicate' and required careful nursing. Was this the first evidence of a 'first-cousin child' problem? The year echoed 1840; Darwin was 'bad and shivery' and again he decamped for much of the summer to Maer and Shrewsbury, where although he was able to do a little work, ill health haunted him. His doctor father did little to help by saying that he thought it would be some years before he became well and strong. As the months wore on, although *The Voyage of the Beagle*, *Coral Reefs* and the Fish volume of the *Zoology of the Voyage of the Beagle* appeared, together with a number of scientific papers, Darwin thought he 'would probably do little more but must be content to admire the strides others make in Science'. He enjoyed and benefited from calls by his scientific colleagues less and less; he came to dislike company, and going out, more and more. On one occasion when he travelled to Maer he started vomiting almost as he got into the house. Meanwhile his evolutionary ideas were developing sporadically; Darwin felt he could not yet confide in his Anglican, establishment friends, particularly the clergymen among them. Perhaps the knowledge that the ideas he was wrestling with were dynamite was the cause of his ill health. Maybe he was quite literally 'sick with worry'.

The illness, difficult to diagnose as it was, the dislike of 'company', the pollution of London, the worry about the allegedly delicate William, all conspired to make him want to get out of detestable, smoky, noisy London. The bolt-holes of Maer and The Mount in Shrewsbury, sometimes on his own, sometimes *en famille*, were all very well, and as we have seen he spent part of several summers in this part of the country. Indeed it was in these two well-loved homes in the early summer of 1842 that he prepared the first draft of his theories. The 'Sketch of 1842', as it has become known, was written in soft pencil on poor-quality paper, entirely so that he could clarify his own mind. But the family sought a more permanent country abode.

London in general and Macaw Cottage in particular were becoming more and more distasteful; Chartist hotheads continued to speak of revolution, or something like it. Demonstrations occurred in London and Manchester. Columns of soldiers marched through the streets of the capital and on at least one occasion they fixed bayonets. There were strikes. The Whiggish Darwins had a certain sympathy for some of the Chartists' aims, but were unhappy about the methods. Charles Darwin craved seclusion and quiet ... and yet there were the scientific institutions of London and colleagues who might be of value to him. He persuaded his father to put up some money for a house, and started to look for a suitable home, something like the vicarages and country rectories that were home to his cousin William Darwin Fox and naturalist colleagues Leonard Jenyns (who wrote much of the Fish volume of *The Zoology of the Voyage of the Beagle*) and John Stevens Henslow (in the Suffolk parish of Hitcham). It needed to be in a rural location, but somewhere between five and twenty miles from a railway station, he thought. He longed for 'pure air, out of the dirt, noise, vice and misery' of London. Kent attracted them, and from time to time in 1841 and 1842 they house-hunted along the chalk downs. In the late summer of 1842 they, with Emma pregnant yet again, bought Down House (no 'e') in the village of Downe (with 'e'), not far from Orpington in Kent. It cost only £2,200, was 'squarish', unpretentious and 'built of shabby bricks'. It had a bit of land. The village had a quiet, rustic charm. It became the Darwin family home from 14 September 1842, until

Emma died in 1896. 'I feel I shall become deeply attached to Down', Charles wrote. And so it proved.

It is unlikely that Charles and Emma felt any great feeling of nostalgia for the two and a half years that they spent on Upper Gower Street. The house was unprepossessing, and although their actual neighbourhood was quiet, London certainly was not. At a time when coal was the main source of energy for heating and cooking the capital was dirty and smoky. There was crime, and the feeling that serious disturbances might break out at any moment. All members of the family were unwell from time to time. Emma was almost continuously pregnant.

But maybe, just maybe, the months at Macaw Cottage played their part in his development. Trying though London life was, Darwin needed those first few years in the capital to make use of the facilities of, and attend the meetings of, the Geological Society, the Zoological Society and other institutions. He was even for a while on the Council of the Royal Geographical Society. He entertained in his own home, and was entertained by the likes of Charles Lyell and Richard Owen (later they would become estranged). Likewise he met the scientific traveller, geographer and geologist Alexander von Humboldt and the botanist de Candolle; he would have been unlikely to do this so readily if he had lived far from London. Thus the difficulties were something that had to be borne so that he was able to establish himself in a network of scientists that would be of such great importance to him later. Perhaps if he had not had such a distaste for the city he would not have moved out to Down House, which was to suit him so well. Maybe, too, the pressures of life in congested, noisy, crime-ridden London, with the hint of conflict not far from the surface, provided an oblique view of Malthusian philosophy, with its emphasis on population growth, competition and struggle.

10

The Down and Up of Family Life

Darwin moved from 12 Upper Gower Street to Down House, Downe, Kent on 17 September 1842, staying on to clear up after Emma and the children had left a few days before. Good news and bad news awaited him and reached him in the first few days of his life at Downe. Emma was well, and liked the place, and Doddy (William), now a toddler, 'was in ecstasies for two whole days'. But Hensleigh wrote from Maer that Josiah Wedgwood (Emma's father and Charles's uncle and long-time supporter; see Chapter 5) was very ill: he seemed to be hallucinating, asking 'whether his father were living, and who was in his place, and what he had died of'. In the event Uncle Jos lived on until July 1843, and Emma, having managed the move well, was delivered of a baby girl, Mary Eleanor, on 23 September, a week after the move. Congratulations flowed in from friends, and Emma made a more rapid recovery than after the births of her previous children. Darwin thought it must be the country air. But poor little Mary did not last long. She died on 16 October, having lived just 23 days: she was buried in the village churchyard.

The other children throve; Doddy, deemed delicate at birth, appeared to be 'much stronger than in London'. His father took an enormous interest in his development, playing with him frequently: he kept a 'baby diary' on his progress, some 40 years later using it as the basis for a paper on child development.

Despite the initial euphoria, there were certain things about the house that were unsatisfactory, and plans for improvements were made almost at once. The central portion of the house (as it now exists) had been built in 1778.

When Charles and Emma moved in, it was said to be dull and unattractive: 'a square brick building of three storeys with shabby whitewash.' The surroundings were open and bleak.

Soon after the family moved in, they had the adjoining lane lowered, and a high flint wall constructed, so that the property was not overlooked; bay windows were built out on the garden side of the house, extending up the entire three storeys; further building work took place in 1843. All this must have been a major source of disturbance for the family during their first few months of occupancy. (A drawing room was added in 1858, and a veranda was constructed on the garden side of this, in 1874: then a new study was built on the front side of the house in 1877.) Nowadays the house gives the impression of a good-sized, but not especially grand, English country house, for the most part whitewashed, somewhat bleak in appearance from the front, but much more attractive, and sheltered by trees, when viewed from the garden to the rear of the property.

This large garden still, in many respects, resembles the garden that Charles Darwin knew, and in which his many children and grandchildren played. One of his daughters, Henrietta (1843–1927, later Mrs Litchfield), recalled:

Many gardens are more beautiful but few could have a greater charm, and nowhere do I know one where it was so pleasant to sit out. The flower-beds were under the drawing room windows, and were filled with hardy herbaceous plants, intermixed with bedded-out plants and annuals. It was often untidy but had a particularly gay and varied effect. On the lawn were two yew-trees where the children had their swing. Beyond the row of lime-trees was the orchard, and a long walk bordered with flowering shrubs let through the kitchen garden to the 'Sand-Walk'. This consisted of a strip of wood planted by my father with varied trees, many being wild cherries and birches, and on one side bordered with hollies. At one end there was a little summer-house and an old pit, out of which the sand was dug which gave it [the path which surrounded the strip of woodland] its name. The walk on one side was always sheltered from the sun and wind, the other sunny, with an outlook over the quiet valley on to the woods beyond, but windy when it blew from the north and east. Here we children played, and here my father took his pacings for forty or more years. (H. Litchfield, *Emma Darwin: a Century of Family Letters, 1792–1896*, 1915, Chapter 5, slightly edited)

20. Down House, from the back garden. This was Charles and Emma Darwin's home for 40 years.

Some of the trees have now gone, but close to the house is a mulberry, said to have been planted in 1609. It was described in Gwen Raverat's (Darwin's granddaughter) account of Down House in the late 1880s and 1890s:

> A great old mulberry tree grew right up against the windows. The shadows of the leaves used to shift about on the white floor, and you could hear the plop of the ripe mulberries as they fell to the ground, and the blackbirds sang there in the early mornings. (Gwen Raverat, *Period Piece*, 1952, Chapter 8)

While Charles Darwin lived at Down House, he to a considerable extent took the part of the village squire, taking an active part in the affairs and institutions of the village. To some extent his demeanour resembled that of his friend John Stevens Henslow, Rector of Hitcham in rural Suffolk, or perhaps his cousin William Fox, in his parish in Cheshire. He did the accounts for village institutions; he dispensed charity. He was on good terms with some (but not all) of the succession of clergy that served the 450 or so souls of the village of Downe. He developed a particularly firm friendship with one, the Reverend John Brodies Innes, which surprised and delighted both of them: sometimes the firmest of friendships can develop between those who disagree strongly in matters of politics and religion. Sometimes he accompanied members of the family who attended the church on the walk thither, without entering himself.

Over the years Charles and Emma attracted a group of household servants, footmen, cooks, maids, nurses, gardeners and governesses, some of whom remained with the family for decades: they were paid adequately but not generously. Sometimes he employed the children of the village to undertake simple tasks for him, such as collecting owl pellets or other specimens. Emma was almost continuously pregnant; child followed child into the world; and book after book, and scientific paper after paper fell from Darwin's pen.

Until the improvements to the 'North Wing' of 1877, Darwin's world centred on the 'old study'. Darwin liked it: 'capital', he called it. It faced the front of the house (for a while a mirror was mounted so that he could see anyone approaching the front door). It measured 18ft × 18ft (approx 5.5m × 5.5m). Wooden shutters could be drawn across the two windows, which

otherwise provided a diffuse, northern light which he found ideal for reading, writing, microscope work or dissecting. A comfortable armchair assisted
clear thinking.

He published his geological studies of *Coral Reefs* (1842) just before
leaving London. From Down came *Volcanic Islands* (1844) and the *Geology
of South America* (1846) followed, completing his *Geology of the Voyage of the
Beagle* triptych. He then devoted seven years to the detailed study of barnacles (1847–54). *On the Origin of Species* was published in 1859, following his
receipt of a letter from Alfred Russel Wallace (see Chapter 12) that contained
the draft of an almost identical theory in 1858. Some of the discussions
(with scientific colleague such as geologist Charles Lyell and botanist Joseph
Hooker) on Charles's own theories took place in the drawing room at Down.
In 1862 there appeared *The Fertilisation of Orchids*, some of the researches for
which were done in a greenhouse in the garden of Down House. *Variation
of Animals and Plants under Domestication* appeared in 1868 and included
work on pigeons undertaken by Darwin at Down. The evolutionary notions
set out in *On the Origin* were picked up and applied to the human species in
The Descent of Man in 1871. Darwin's last book, *The Formation of Vegetable
Mould through the Action of Worms* (1881), has a special association with
Down House; it contains numerous detailed observations made in the Down
garden, some made very soon after the family moved in. Not far from the
house is the 'worm stone', a device put there to measure the rate at which the
activities of earthworms buried a large circular block.

A railway station just a few miles away allowed him to attend scientific
meetings in London. There were occasional family excursions (e.g. the Great
Exhibition of 1851, which was much enjoyed), visits to relatives (especially
Maer and Shrewsbury) and holidays. At certain times Darwin went for
medical treatment to hydropathic spas such as those of Dr James Gully in
Malvern and Dr Edward Lane at Moor Park. Some years he went to meetings
of the British Association for the Advancement of Science – held in the late
summer, in a different city each year. It is not true, as he once claimed, that
he 'never went anywhere', but the statement that he and Emma led a 'retired
life' is probably fair.

After poor Mary came (and went) in 1842, offspring followed one another in quick succession. Henrietta Emma arrived in 1843, George Howard in 1845, then Elizabeth in 1847, and Francis in 1848. There was a very slightly longer interval before Leonard joined the family in 1850. Horace followed very soon after in 1851. Charles Waring was the last in 1856, arriving when Emma was approaching fifty.

In some ways it was the very ideal of upper-middle-class Victorian family life. Charles Darwin played joyously with his children, took an interest in the affairs of the village squire, and pottered round his 'thinking walk' – the Sandwalk. A little surprisingly he was sworn in as a magistrate, perhaps hoping to identify more closely with other village squires in the county, in 1857. He had his father's, grandfather's and father-in-law's fortunes behind him.

He took a great interest in his children's activities and schooling, encouraging any glimmer of interest in science wherever it appeared. There appeared in a journal called the *Entomologist's Weekly Intelligencer* for 25 June 1859 (a matter of weeks before the publication of *On the Origin*) a note recording the capture of several rather rare species of beetle, purporting to have been written by three of Charles Darwin's sons (Horace, Francis and Leonard). The note commences: 'We are three very young collectors having lately taken in the Parish of Downe …'. As the boys were then aged from about eight to twelve years, it seems unlikely that they had much to do with the writing of the note, although they may have helped by capturing the creatures concerned. All three became scientists of one kind or another, so perhaps history repeated itself: with them as with their father, the youthful apparently random collection of beetles led to more systematic enquiries later.

But happy incidents such as this concealed an anxiety, almost a melancholia. Occasionally he seems to have worried about money, although he would seem to have little need to do so. Sometimes he expressed his concern about the costs of educating his large family, especially the boys. William took up photography, which was an expensive hobby.

Darwin suffered ill health – more or less chronically – from the ages of about 30 to 60. There seems to have been some improvement in the final decade of his life: this last would seem to argue against an organic origin (such as some infection picked up in South America, the Pacific Islands or South Africa) for his poor health. From his own and other accounts, symptoms during this period seem to have included flatulence, stomach acidity, vomiting, shivering, fainting ('dying sensations'), blurred vision, dots before the eyes, ringing in the ears, over-excitement at the prospect of meeting groups of people, skin eruptions or eczema. He often felt tired, and sometimes he felt only able to do a few hours of work a day.

Some recent thinking suggests that much of Darwin's ill health was largely psychogenetic. Da Costa's syndrome (or hyperventilation syndrome, or anxiety disorder) has been mentioned. Both physiological and psychological factors are involved.

The immediate cause of symptoms may be an increase in the level of anxiety, or fear, associated with an increase in breathing, without any increase in activity or energy use. When an animal experiences fear or anxiety, often increased oxygen intake occurs, as it prepares for 'fight or flight'. In the absence of such activity (and the associated energy consumption), the increased unstable breathing leads to a lowering of, and fluctuations in, the level of carbon dioxide in the blood. Persistent overbreathing may cause the carbon dioxide level to remain at a level slightly above that at which symptoms are produced. Any situation, even if quite trivial (animated conversation, or meeting with a group of people, might be sufficient, or on the other hand, simply being left alone for a period), can trigger symptoms. These symptoms may cause further worry and arousal; the patient may believe that he has some defect of the stomach or heart. He may feel that he will become very ill or die; this may perhaps lead to what might be called a panic attack. A vicious circle may ensue.

The intensity of Darwin's symptoms varied. He seems to have had health problems immediately before sailing on the *Beagle*; they seem to have recurred again in September 1837 (shortly after his conversion to an evolutionary outlook) and when he was working very hard on writing up the material from the voyage, at the end of 1839 just before the birth of his first child; symptoms seem to have continued through into the early 1840s, when the real structure of his evolutionary conspectus was taking shape. At that time he was good friends with Richard Owen, Zoologist at the College of Surgeons. They had meals together, and often met at the meetings of the Geological Society. But to be faced with such affability while developing his own 'transmutationist' notions, knowing that Owen had publicly castigated Lamarck's ideas, and was firmly, and outspokenly, within the traditional mould and opposed to such notions, must have been a source of tension in Darwin, and it may have been this that made him ill. Attendance at meetings induced illness, leaving him 'knocked up' the following day.

Other incidents seem to have occurred in 1848 and 1849, around the time of his father's final illness and death; and again in 1863 to 1864, three years or so after the publication of *On the Origin*, as opposition grew.

It has thus been argued that it was during periods of overwork, and in times of stress or great anxiety, that Darwin's illness became worse. The situation was perhaps aggravated by the fact that, just as Charles was convinced he was an invalid, so his wife Emma seemed to be more than happy to nurse him. The more Emma pandered to his worries, the more convinced Charles was that he was unwell! His granddaughter, Gwen Raverat, in *Period Piece* maintained that there was a family tradition of hypochondria! A related suggestion is that because of the loss of his mother at the age of seven years, and the sometimes rather strained relationship he had with his father, Charles was 'predisposed' to psychological problems and depression (see Chapter 3).

All manner of treatments were prescribed by a platoon of medical advisers: a bland diet was suggested, but also the consumption of plenty of wine; abstention from snuff (a popular distraction in the nineteenth century, and one of which the young Darwin was rather fond); being wrapped in zinc or brass wires moistened with vinegar; hydroelectric chains; a range of patent medicines. Sometimes he was wrapped in cold, wet cloths, or given cold baths. Surprisingly he expressed the opinion that some of these helped him: perhaps the tortures just took his mind off some of his other worries.

Darwin could certainly afford the best medical advice. Charles received assets worth some £40,000 on the death of his father. He was left a second farm in Lincolnshire (he already owned one), as well as several private mortgages.

Emma, besides her interest in the family pottery firm, held shares in the expanding railway and (by now perhaps past their peak) canal companies. Their cautious nature also favoured investments in government bonds. In the 1850s their combined income approached a very substantial £5,000 per year. Frequently Charles was able to re-invest about half of his income.

Sometimes Wedgwood children came to stay, and on occasion there were about a dozen children romping round the house and garden. There were outings to Knole Park, near Sevenoaks. Sometimes the Wedgwood family reciprocated, and there were outings for bilberry picking at Leith Hill, close to the home of one branch of the family. Charles enjoyed their company, even if he found the occasional pandemonium stressful. Annie particularly enjoyed the company of the visitors, and after they left following a visit in the summer of 1850 she was disconsolate for some weeks. Emma and Charles began to be worried: could it be that first-cousin marriages really were dangerous? Eldest daughter, cheerful, bright, intelligent Annie was a special favourite of Charles. She had grey eyes, and long brown hair: she was particularly affectionate to adults. She used to accompany her father on his quiet potterings around the Sandwalk. In the latter part of 1850 Annie began to find her lessons a burden. She had headaches and was feverish. A dose of flu that ran through the family early in 1851 did not help. At the end of March 1851 Charles and Emma resolved to take her to see Dr Gully, in Malvern, who had earlier subjected Charles to one of his water-treatments, apparently with benign results. Charles took her there, leaving her with one of his sisters, then left for London to see some of his scientific colleagues, and then returned to Down House. But on 15 April he received an urgent summons from Malvern. Annie was deteriorating. She was very feverish and vomiting: she had lost weight. Charles hurried back and was overcome by the appearance of his dear, weakening child. In regular despatches to Emma he described the 'struggle between life and death'. At times Dr Gully was optimistic, but her pulse was weak and she had lost control of her bladder, and had serious diarrhoea. But then she took a little food and Dr Gully pronounced himself pleased. Charles's mood soared and sank by turns: 'the alternations … sicken the soul,' he wrote to Emma, heavily pregnant at home at Downe. He went on: 'I wish you could see her, the perfection of gentleness, patience and gratitude … poor dear little soul.' The bedside vigil took its toll on Charles and he collapsed into illness too. The sinking continued, and little Annie was unconscious for long periods. Anne Elizabeth Darwin died at midday on 23 April 1851, possibly from tuberculosis.

Charles Darwin did not think he could bear the funeral: he hurried home to his weeping, grief-stricken Emma. Just a few close relatives and Down House servants attended the graveside rites; she was buried beneath a cedar tree in the nearby Priory churchyard. Her epitaph reads: 'A dear and good child'.

Charles wrote an emotional 'memorial' to her, in which he described her as 'the joy of the household'. He mentioned also her 'buoyant joyousness' and her sensitivity. She was, he stated, neat in dress, charming, nimble with her hands, artistic and musical. Even allowing for the possible exaggeration of a grief-stricken parent she does seem to have been a delightful and model child. Her death profoundly affected the family. Neither Charles nor Emma ever fully got over the loss, and the other children were distraught.

The opinion has also been expressed that the death of his dearest child was an important incident in Charles's journey towards evolutionary ideas. It may have shattered what remained of his Christian faith – no longer could he believe in a loving God and a moral universe – and so he was able to more boldly make the intellectual leap towards evolutionary ideas. It also brought home to him yet again that death was a natural phenomenon – a part of life. He was always concerned both that his children might inherit his own ill health, and that marriage to cousins was deleterious, reducing the possibility of the combination of characteristics from different ancestries (this was long before the nature of genes was understood). Heredity was an important component in natural selection, so it may be that the combination of thoughts and feelings that Annie's death aroused may have nudged him in the direction of his notions of natural selection and the 'survival of the fittest'. Certainly in the months following her death Charles concentrated fully on his 'species theory'.

But, following the tragedy, in many respects life went on. The Victorian sunshine, it seemed, frequently shone on the family at Downe. Charles worked on his various scientific projects – in his study, in the greenhouse. During periods of better health he went to scientific meetings in London; when he was not so well he wandered round his Sandwalk. His acquaintanceship with the leading scientific figures of the day – Joseph Hooker, Charles Lyell, Thomas Huxley – became deeper, and he ventured to test his revolutionary ideas on them. Sometimes they came to stay at Down House, as did Charles's bachelor brother Erasmus, to the great joy of the family. The boys went off to school … and came home … and then went off to university (Cambridge of course; by the late 1850s his son William was occupying his old rooms at Christ's College). The family continued to be attended upon by a group of loyal servants. Emma was busy with household and family, but sometimes read to Charles, or soothed him by playing the piano.

Horace had been born close to the time of dear little Annie's death, and Charles and Emma expected this baby to be the last. But five years later, as Charles began writing up his species theory, she was pregnant again, and by mid-year the nausea that had accompanied her earlier pregnancies dogged her once more. Charles Waring Darwin was born shortly before Christmas 1856: it soon became clear quite that he was not normal, and had been born 'without [his] … full share of intelligence'. He was affectionate and smiled a lot but was very backward in talking or walking. It is quite likely that he suffered Down's Syndrome (which was not recognized until a few years later). This syndrome, which is due to a chromasomal abnormality, occurs, on average, in about 1 in 800 live births. However, the probability of giving birth to a Down's child increases from 1 in 1,490 at maternal age 20 to 24, to about 1 in 60 at age 40. By age 49 (Emma's age), the probability is 1 in 11. Recent research also suggests that the age of the father, especially beyond 42, also increases the risk of the abnormality manifesting in pregnancies in older mothers. The probability of Emma and Charles, both nearing 50, having a Down's child would now be considered very high indeed.

Down's children also seem to be liable to infection, and in the summer of 1858 scarlet fever was rampant in the village of Downe: six children eventually died. Poor Charles Waring passed away on the evening of 28 June 1858, and in a memorial his father wrote:

Our poor little darling's short life has been placid, innocent and joyful. I think &
trust he did not suffer so much at last ... but the last 36 hours were miserable beyond
expression. In the sleep of Death he resumed his placid expression.

Immediately after the baby's funeral, the remainder of the children were
sent away to stay with relatives. Charles noted that it had been a miserable
couple of weeks, but it went on: his sister Marianne died a few days later.
His daughter Henrietta was unwell. Again he wondered whether first-cousin
marriages were the source of many of the family's problems. There had by
now been four Wedgwood–Darwin marriages, and he and Emma might have
felt that they had run out of luck.

But as he and Emma pulled their life together following the death of their
tenth child; they had other matters to consider.

11

The Dawning of Dangerous Ideas

We have noted (in Chapter 7) that Darwin was not only extremely fortunate in the variety of environments, organisms and human societies that he saw while he was a-voyaging on HMS *Beagle*, but also in the order in which he saw them. He was 'able to make out' the relatively straightforward geology of the Cape Verde Islands before he came to the complexities of the Falkland Islands, Tierra del Fuego and the Andes. He described the simple network of ecological relationships on St Paul's before he was overwhelmed by the tropical forests of Brazil. Developing his coral atoll theory as the ship rolled its way across the Pacific, he was able to put the finishing touches to it in the week at the beautiful atoll of Cocos in the Indian Ocean. Also he saw the to him primitive society of Tierra del Fuego, before the apparently more advanced communities of Tahiti and New Zealand. Interestingly, late in the voyage he arranged the near-naked Fuegans, the Maoris, the Tahitians and other races he encountered as ascending points on a ladder or scale of advancement.

It is often asserted that the five and a half weeks in the Galapagos Islands (April to May 1835) were pivotal. Darwin himself, however, in his *Autobiography*, recalled:

> During the voyage of the *Beagle* I had been deeply impressed ... by the South American character of most of the productions of the Galapagos archipelago, and more especially by the manner in which they differ slightly on each island of the group; none of these islands appearing very old in a geological sense.

But a careful scrutiny of the archives reveals there was no sudden insight

while he was in the Galapagos. Although Darwin was deeply impressed by
the archipelago, and made important observations there, it was only later –
indeed, some months after his return to England – that he was 'converted'
to an evolutionary outlook. While actually on the islands he was uncertain
about which region it was to which they had closest biological affinities. He
was puzzled on seeing seals, penguins, palms and tropical birds in the same
environment. Darwin's recollections in the *Autobiography*, written late in his
life, well over 40 years after the event, appear either to be mistaken or perhaps
to give an incorrect impression.

In fact Darwin spent only 19 days, in some cases only in part, on land in
the Galapagos archipelago. The remainder of the time he was aboard the
ship as she made her way between the islands while engaged in hydrographic
survey work. He only landed on four of the islands, although he had good
views of another eight.

There were many aspects of the archipelago he did not like.

> These islands at a distance have a sloping uniform outline, excepting where broken
> by sundry paps & hillocks; the whole black Lava, *completely* covered by small leafless
> brushwood & low trees. The fragments of Lava where most porous, are reddish like
> cinders; the stunted trees show little signs of life. The black rocks heated by the rays
> of the Vertical sun, like a stove, give to the air a close & sultry feeling. The plants
> also smell unpleasantly. The country was compared to what we might imagine the
> cultivated parts of the Infernal regions to be. (*Diary*, 15 September 1835)

Negative adjectives predominate: small, leafless, low, stunted, little, close,
sultry, unpleasant[ly], Infernal. The appearance of some of the reptiles disgusted him. A couple of days later, his diary records:

> The black Lava rocks on the beach are frequented by large (2–3 ft) most disgusting,
> clumsy Lizards. They are as black as the porous rocks over which they crawl & seek
> their prey from the Sea. Somebody calls them 'imps of darkness'. They assuredly well
> become the land they inhabit. When on shore I proceeded to botanize & obtained 10
> different flowers; but such insignificant, ugly little flowers, as would better become
> an Arctic than a Tropical country.

It was only when he was able to discuss his bird specimens from the islands (and those of his shipmates who had taken specimens) with naturalists in London that he understood the significance of the differences between them. Indeed he made a number of errors while collecting in the Galapagos. He 'intermingled' specimens from different islands. And it was only fairly late in his sojourn that he realized that the shells of the famous Galapagos tortoises differed from one island to another. Some of these great creatures were taken aboard the ship to provide meat for the long voyage ahead, but the shells were cast overboard after the meat was consumed. Darwin almost literally let important evidence for evolution 'slip through his hands'!

A case may be made for saying that the two Falklands visits (1833 and 1834) were just as significant, or even more so, as the sojourn in the Galapagos. He spent more time there (a little less than ten weeks, in total), he covered more pages with notes, and certainly, of some categories, collected more specimens.

Some of the conclusions that Darwin reached as the result of his explorations in the Falklands were extremely important in themselves, but as is so often the case it was comparisons that were important. It was the fact that the young naturalist was able to compare the bleak windswept environments of East Falkland with those of the tropical islands, the biota of the Falkands with those of Tierra del Fuego and mainland South America, and the 'continental' rocks (quartzites and sandstones for example) of East Falkland with the lavas and ashes of some of his volcanic islands, that was vital to him. Darwin had the knack of comparison: 'The habit of comparison leads to generalisation,' he wrote towards the end of the voyage.

Within the island there were startling comparisons to be seen. He compared the bleak, open moorlands with the nearby kelp beds (see pages 55, 57), that were teeming with life. He also appreciated the integrity of the whole environment, spending hours studying the organisms that made up the kelp communities in Berkeley Sound. He wrote the following account in April 1834, combining material from his two sojourns at East Falkland, but drawing in material from similar observations he had made in Tierra del Fuego:

The Zoology of the Sea is I believe the same here as in Tierra del Fuego: Its main striking feature is the immense quantity & number of aquatic beings which are intimately connected with the Kelp. The plant ... is universally attached to rocks, from those which are awash at low water & those being in fathom water: it is frequently attached to round stones lying in mud. From the degree to which these southern lands are intersected by water & the depth in which Kelp grows the quantity may be imagined ... I can only compare these giant forests to terrestrial ones in the most teeming part of the Tropics; yet if the latter in any country were to be destroyed, I do not believe nearly the same number of animals (a) would perish, as would happen in the case of the Kelp: All the fishing quadrupeds & birds (& man) haunt the beds attracted by the infinite number of small fish which live amongst the leaves: (the kinds are not so very numerous, my specimens I believe show nearly all.) Amongst the invertebrates I will mention them in order of their importance. Crustacea of every order swarm, my collection gives no idea of them, especially the minute sorts. Encrusting Corallines & Aztias are excessively numerous. Every leaf (excepting those on the surface) is white with such Corallines ... & compound Ascidia. Examining these with a strong microscope minute crustacea will be seen. ... On shaking the great entangled roots it is curious to see the heap of fish, shells, crabs, sea-eggs, cuttlefish, star fish, Planaria, Nercilae which fall out. This latter tribe I have much neglected. Amongst the Gasteropoda [sic], Herobranchus is common: but Trochus & patelliform shells abound on all the leaves. One single plant forms an immense and most interesting menagerie. If this Fucus was to cease living, with it would go many of the Seals, the Cormorants & certainly the small fish & sooner or later the Fuegan Man must follow. The greater number of invertebrates would likewise perish, but how many it is hard to conjecture.

A later note refers to the '(a)' added in small handwriting to the text, perhaps when Darwin looked over his work sometime later. It reads: 'I refer to numbers of individuals as well as kinds.'

This description reveals how insightful Darwin had become in evaluating environments by April 1834 (about halfway through the voyage). He has clearly compared the beds of East Falkland with those of Tierra del Fuego; moreover there are several important ecological concepts embedded in the account. Darwin is comparing the *productivity* of the kelp beds with that of the tropical rainforests he had recently seen in Brazil. He distinguishes carefully between number of individuals (*population*) and number of species (*diversity*). He comes close to using the concepts (but not the terms): *food chain, food web, ecological niche* and *dominant* or maybe *keystone species*. He stresses that humans (man, 'Fuegan man') are part of the system: they interact with, and form part of, the environment in a way very comparable with that of other creatures. The young Charles Darwin is describing an environment – a modern biologist would say *ecosystem* – in a strikingly holistic and integrated manner. Later the notion of an organism being intimately linked to its environment was to reappear in the concept of natural selection.

But he was analytical, as well as integrative. He studied the various species of plants and animals that make up the Falkland Islands' relatively simple land biota. Some of them, especially some of the plants, were the same as on Tierra del Fuego. He speculated as to the mechanisms of dispersal. 'The plants and insects might easily be transported from Tierra del [Fuego] in the furious SW gales,' he thought. But as he watched flocks of wild geese feeding on the tussac grass he wondered whether migrating birds might carry seeds from the mainland of South America. Metaphorical seeds were also being sown in Darwin's mind. As, decades later, he was to point out in *On the Origin of Species*, if all life was ultimately derived from a few simple forms, it follows that all the organisms now extant on remote islands must be derived from ancestors that made their way thither by some process of *long-distance dispersal*.

But some of the animals were endemic – unique, found nowhere else – he thought. Such was the Falklands fox, or warrah (modern scientific name *Dusicyon australis*). Moreover, when he compared specimens of this creature, they differed according to which island they came from. Those from West Falkland were smaller and darker in the colour of their fur compared to those from East Falkland.

Darwin constantly reworked his notes throughout the voyage. He annotated the notes from one location with comparisons from another site. Sometimes he rewrote a set of notes completely, as new information came to light, and as new ideas came into his mind.

Some notes, dated by some scholars at June 1836, when the *Beagle* was on

21. The warrah, Falklands fox or Falklands wolf. Extinct since the late nineteenth century. Darwin noted that the fur of the animals in West Falkland and East Falkland differed, long before he visited the Galapagos. *From the Mammals volume (ii) of* The Zoology of the Voyage of the Beagle

her homeward run, make interesting comparisons between the Falklands and the Galapagos that were visited many months later:

> When I see these Islands in sight of each other … possessed of but a scanty stock of animals, tenanted by these birds, but slightly differing in structure & filling the same place in Nature [i.e. occupying a similar ecological niche], I must suspect they are only varieties. The only fact of a similar kind of which I am aware, is the constantly asserted difference – between the wolf-like Fox of East & West Falkland Islds. – If there is the slightest foundation for these remarks the zoology of Archipelagoes – will be well worth examining: for such facts would undermine the stability of Species. (Darwin's Notes, Cambridge University Library)

Although this was very late in the voyage, it does not seem that Darwin was at this time a *convinced* transmutationist. (Indeed some say that these writings were made later, after his return.) But it does seem that he may have been very vaguely, perhaps, entertaining the possibility of instability of species: a possibility which is raised, but immediately dismissed, by Charles Lyell in Volume II of *Principles of Geology*, which Darwin had been reading and rereading.

But not only did Charles Darwin compare the plants and animals of the Falklands with those of other islands and archipelagoes, and the different habitats within the island group, he also compared the organisms of the Falklands of the nineteenth century with those of the remote past:

> I was … surprised to find … beds of sandstone which abounded with impressions and casts of shells. The sandstone is fine grained and soft: it is often slaty, in which case it generally contains scales of mica … The included organic remains are found in seams or beds between the sandstone strata. In some cases the casts form the whole mass, in others they are embedded in sandstone, and very often in a matrix of … compact rock. The shells belong to Terebratula and its subgenera; there are also species of Entrochitus and vestiges of some other remains the nature of which I could not ascertain. (Darwin's Notes, Cambridge University Library)

Darwin wondered about the exact age of the fossils (they are now thought to be from the Devonian period, and about 350 to 400 million years old), and how they compared with fossils of similar age from other parts of the world.

The stratum from which Darwin collected is indeed extremely fossiliferous: it contains dozens of species fossils, of brachiopods, crinoids and trilobites. Darwin's phrase 'abounding with shells' is entirely appropriate. He noted particularly the contrast with the landscape that surrounded him, bleak and infertile. Over the whole island, he recorded there was '[t]he same entire absence of trees & the same universal covering of brown wiry grass'. It was very monotonous and there were few land insects or other invertebrates. Darwin compared the cold, bleak environment of the modern Falkland Islands with the prolific seas, perhaps experiencing a much warmer climate, that might have existed in the geological past when the sandstones 'abounding with shells' were deposited. Environments had changed throughout geological time.

22. Fossils from East Falkland. Darwin's whole opinion of the desolate archipelago changed when he found a sandstone 'abounding with shells'. This specimen was collected from close to Darwin's location. *Geography Department, University of Western Australia*

There were other fossils that he collected during the voyage that proved important to him.

On 22 September 1832, Darwin went on a 'very pleasant cruize [*sic*] with the Captain and Lieut. Sulivan' at Punta Alta, on the coast of Patagonia. The 'Philos' was poking around in the cliffs and found some 'very interesting' fossils. They included 'numerous shells & the bones of large animals'. He had got the bit between his teeth and returned to the same site the following day, and

> To my great joy, I found the head of some large animal, imbedded in the soft rock. It took me three hours to get it out. As far as I am able to judge, it is allied to the Rhinoceros. I did not get it on board till some hours after it was dark. (*Diary*, 23 September 1832)

Other fossils came later, both from this site and from others. From the same low cliffs just over a fortnight after his first visit:

> I obtained a jaw bone, which contained a tooth: by this I found that it belongs to the great ante-diluvial animal the Megatherium ['giant animal']. This is particularly interesting as the only specimens in Europe are in the King's collection at Madrid, where for all purposes of science they are as nearly as much hidden as if in their primaeval rock.

He wrote a few days later to Professor Henslow in Cambridge. He referred to his 'luck in collecting', going on: 'I have been very lucky with fossil bones.' Some of the animals were very large and several of them were new to science, he asserted. He believed he had found the remains of giant sloths, a giant armadillo and an enormous rodent. Later he found, in a farmyard, the bones of a fossil llama. Yes, Darwin was fortunate. But he was diligent, returning again and again to good sites, and seeking out others, and spending many hours excavating his specimens. He crated them up and sent them off.

By the end of the voyage, Charles Darwin had landed on nearly 40 islands (counting Australia and Tasmania as two), and glimpsed a number from afar. He had explored the biological diversity of Brazil's tropical rainforests, and the deserts and scrublands of Patagonia and South Africa. He had compared the tropical forests with the very different forests of Australia, New Zealand

and the southern part of South America. He had ascended the Andes, collecting fossils from high altitudes. He had noted evidence for sea-level change in South America and several other parts of the world. He had experienced an earthquake, seen the effects of a tsunami, and clambered up mountains and waded out to sea on coral reefs. He had collected and observed a wide variety of sea life. He had met with Australian Aborigines, South American Indians, Fuegans, Maoris and Tahitians.

In his development of his Coral Atoll Theory, and comparisons of the organisms from different islands and his speculations about long-distance oceanic dispersal, he was becoming more confident as a theoretician. Applying techniques learnt from Sedgwick in North Wales, coupled with his reading of Lyell's *Principles of Geology*, he was able to reconstruct past environments, and appreciate that he lived in a dynamic, changing world.

Yes, he had the most fantastic luck in the places he visited. But he knew how to make use of his good fortune in diligent fieldwork, repeated observations, careful note-taking and 'the habit of comparison'.

Landing at Falmouth in early October 1836, he proceeded by rapid stage-coaches to Shrewsbury and his welcoming family (see Chapter 6, page 63, Chapter 8, page 93). After just a few days in Shropshire he hurried to Cambridge and the Henslows. Then to London, then back to Cambridge. He scuttled from institution to institution – the College of Surgeons, the Zoological Society, the Geological Society, the British Museum, the Linnean Society. He himself said that he was working harder than ever before. Not himself a specialist taxonomist for any biological group, he needed to find those who would look after his specimens – thousands of them – and classify and describe them, and help him to understand their significance. In due course Richard Owen took the fossil mammals, Henslow himself looked at some of the plants, and Henslow's brother-in-law Leonard Jenyns did a very good job on the fishes. John Gould took on the birds, but departed for Australia before the task was quite complete. Thomas Bell, the new Zoology Professor at King's College, London, took over the mammals, and George R. Waterhouse the reptiles and amphibians and also some of the insects, his son F. H. Waterhouse dealing with some of the remaining insects. The Sowerby brothers (for a fee) took over the mollusc shells and later did illustrative work. John Morris and Daniel Sharpe, members of the Geological Society, looked at the fossils from the Falkland Islands. One can see strong evidence of the Cambridge Network in this list: friends and relatives of persons whom Darwin had got to know at Cambridge figure prominently (see Chapter 4). The time the undergraduate Charles Darwin spent at Henslow's soirées had not been wasted. Darwin managed to get government funding to assist with the publication of *The Zoology of the Voyage of the Beagle*, and cooperated closely with the individual experts. Brief examples of his dependence on this by now expanding circle will be given.

The ornithologist and artist John Gould held the poorly paid position of 'Animal preserver' at the Zoological Society, but he developed a sideline in the production of beautifully illustrated books on birds. He carefully examined Darwin's Galapagos birds. There was in fact a single group of small birds – 'a series of ground finches which are so peculiar'. They varied in the shape of their beaks and in certain other regards, but were in fact closely related, and had South American connections. The mockingbirds that Darwin had collected on the Galapagos, too, told a similar story. These, in contrast with some of his other specimens, Darwin *had* labelled by their specific island source. There were three species, closely related, and also linked to South American birds. Thomas Bell told him that the iguanas also varied from island to island. And then there was that recollected information about the shells of the tortoises being different on each island .... By mid-March 1837 Charles Darwin had put together in his own mind the facts that the Galapagos Islands were relatively recent geologically; that many animals had arrived from South America (the nearest continental mainland); and that the arrivals had somehow changed and now presented a diversity of new species.

Meanwhile Owen had confirmed Darwin's idea of a giant sloth, a giant armadillo and fragments of a gigantic llama. There was no rhinoceros, nor elephant. The fossil animals seemed to be the precursors – sometimes the giant precursors – of animals found in South America today. Could they be linked by descent?

On 14 March 1837 Darwin accompanied John Gould to a meeting of the Geological Society at which Gould discussed the 'ostriches' (rheas) that Darwin had collected in South America. There were two species, with differing distributions: it was as though they had agreed to split the South American plains between them. His observations on the distribution of the two species, and the similarity of their forms, led him to wonder whether they might have had a common ancestor.

Darwin had opened his Red Notebook around the time he departed from Australia in March 1836, and had been filling it with ideas, references – random thoughts almost – ever since. In this notebook appear what seem to be Darwin's first writings on transmutation of species, or evolution. And they refer to the rheas, or 'ostriches' on page 127:

> Speculate on neutral ground of 2 ostriches; bigger one encroaches on smaller: – change not progressive: produced at one blow ...

A couple of pages later he compares the relationship between the two ostrich species in space with that between the llamas in time:

> Should urge that extinct Llama owed its death not to change of circumstances ...
>   The same kind of relation that the common ostrich bears to (Pettisse ...) [the other smaller species]: extinct Guanaco [llama] to recent: in former case position, in latter time. (or changes consequent on lapse) being the relation. – As in first case distinct species inosculate, so must we believe ancient ones: not gradual change or degeneration. from circumstances: if one species does change into another it must be per saltum – or species may perish. = This [inosculation *deleted*] representation of species important, each its own limit & represented.

This needs a little decoding. Darwin is suggesting that the relationship between the 'common ostrich' (i.e. the greater or common rhea, *Rhea americana*) and the 'Petisse' (the lesser rhea, Darwin's rhea, *Pterocnemia pennata*, formerly known by the scientific name *Rhea darwinii*), which had two distinct distributions in South America, is in some ways analogous to that between the extinct llama or 'Guanaco' and the modern form. In both cases, Darwin seems to be speculating that they might have a common ancestor: he uses the word 'inosculate', a medical term (perhaps picked up in Edinburgh Medical School days) used for the joining or branching of blood vessels. However, he seems to be thinking in terms of a sudden or *saltatory* change for he uses the words '*per saltum*' (by a leap, in fits and starts) and 'produced at one blow'. At this early stage in Darwin's development his notion of evolution seems to be closer to the 'punctuated equilibrium' of Stephen Jay Gould in the late twentieth century. His gradualist approach to evolution developed later. Lyell's notion that the past sometimes explains the present could be extended from the geological realm to the biological.

The first few weeks of March 1837 were perhaps the most important in the aspiring naturalist's life. Working with the likes of Owen and Gould, relying on his fossil specimens, and the bird skins and other zoological specimens that he (and some of his shipmates) had collected, suddenly he was a transmutationist. The word *conversion* has been used. The coincidence of a few individuals in London together with the appropriate specimens at the same time was uniquely serendipitous.

Although he did not widely broadcast the nature of his dangerous idea, Darwin had passed the turning point. Possibly the Red Notebook was filled by about May 1837; some of the themes he develops within it are taken up by later notebooks in the period 1837 to 1839. Notebook A followed up some of the geological themes discussed in the Red Notebook; Notebook B was opened in mid-July 1837 (it was followed by C, D and E) and in this he continued to record his thoughts and speculations on the 'species question' or transmutation. Early in one of these is a simple branching diagram – like a twig with several stems growing out of it – intended to show the genealogical relationships. This represented another milestone.

Darwin realized that his ideas were subversive, and by many conservative Christians would be regarded as heretical. The notion of humans as having descended from lower forms of life ran in the face of the orthodox view of 'Man created in the image of God'. If life begat life the very notion of a Creating God might wither. The paternalistic notion of a created world with each organism occupying its allocated place, and by extension, each human being filling his or her appropriate role, was put in danger. Cecil Frances

Alexander's (1818–95) early Victorian hymn in praise of a God that created
a bounteous and beautiful natural world begins:

> All things bright and beauteous,
> All creatures great and small,
> All things wise and wondrous,
> The Lord God made them all.
> Each little flower that opens,
> Each little bird that sings,
> He made their glowing colours,
> He made their tiny wings.

But it continues:

> The rich man in his castle,
> The poor man at his gate,
> GOD made them, high or lowly,
> And ordered their estate.

(Some readers may know a slightly different version of this ever-popular
hymn; the above appears to be the original version, written in 1848.)

It was not just the order of nature that was ordained by the Creator, but the
very structure and ordering of society.

Transmutationist ideas had already made their appearance. Darwin's
Edinburgh teacher, Dr Grant, was one early advocate. Jean-Baptiste Lamarck
(1744–1829) was French and therefore suspect; but Charles's grandfather
Erasmus Darwin (1731–1802) was an Englishman, and a distinguished one
at that. Erasmus had put forward evolutionary ideas in *Zoönomia* (1796):
his grandson had read this and moreover had inscribed the title on one of
his transmutation notebooks. The commanding heights of Science were
held by Anglicans. Adam Sedgwick referred to 'infidel naturalists' (although,
geologist that he was, he did certainly not believe that the earth was just a
few thousand years old). Richard Owen was a conservative Anglican layman,
and was another enemy of radical views. He believed that the similarity in
the forms, for example, of the vertebrates was due to their being designed
to the same blueprint or *archetype*. This archetype was an idea in the Divine

Mind. But Owen was also Darwin's collaborator in the Fossil Mammals volume, and they met regularly. Even his good friend Charles Lyell was sceptical: the idea of humans being descended from apes, for example, he said brutalized the 'high estate' of humanity. Radical scientific views were held to signify atheism, and atheism was anent to treason. Atheism, anarchy and social disintegration had gone together in the France of the eighteenth century. Heaven forbid that history would repeat itself in the England of the nineteenth.

Darwin knew he had to be careful: and he was.

12

The Origin of the Origin

Charles Darwin, during his time at Downe, and indeed before, engaged in a prolific correspondence, seeking information to bolster his species theory and information for his many other (often related) research projects. Over 14,000 letters (some 7,600 sent and over 6,530 received according to one recent count) are known, and new letters are continuing to be discovered at the rate of several dozen a year. Sometimes Darwin wrote several letters a day. On each of Christmas Eve and Christmas Day 1859 he wrote three letters. The record seems to be New Year's Day 1874, when he wrote 12 letters. No doubt many hundreds of letters have been lost or destroyed. Several times in the last few decades of his life he sent and received over 300 letters in a year; it has been computed that he wrote an average of 0.59 letters per day during this period. He usually replied to letters promptly. Perhaps the most important reason for this apparent profligacy was that postal communication became practicable and inexpensive with the introduction of Britain's 'penny postage' in 1840, four years after Darwin's return from the *Beagle* voyage. Previously postage had been much more expensive, and had usually been paid by the person receiving a letter. In this way, the study at Down House was linked to the scientific world. History would have been very different if it had not been so.

Moreover, the railways, on which this efficient postal system in part depended, expanded rapidly in the early Victorian period. George Stephenson had applied the new technology to his Stockton and Darlington Railway in 1825, although horses were still employed. The first truly successful steam railway was the Liverpool and Manchester Railway, which opened in 1830. The L&M sparked a feverish boom in railway building that lasted 20 years. By 1854 every town of any consequence in England was connected to the railway network. At the same time steamships were opening up international travel: it was possible to receive a reply to an administrator, missionary or military officer in some distant part of the Empire within a reasonable time.

Charles Darwin, and indeed British Science in general, was remarkably fortunate that new ideas were being developed and tested, new museums and institutions expanding at exactly the time when communication between scientists, and the exchange of specimens and ideas, was becoming easier and cheaper.

In the years following his 'Eureka moment' in the spring of 1837, he was hard at work quietly developing his ideas, and collecting evidence for them. While he was working on the book that became known as *The Voyage of the Beagle*, and the three volumes of the *Geology of the Voyage*, supervising the five volumes of the *Zoology of the Voyage*, and preparing his great tomes on barnacles, the transmutation notebooks were gradually filling. He was gathering information, examples and ideas from all parts of the world. Letters to Charles Lyell elicited information on geology and to Joseph Hooker on botany. (Hooker travelled the southern hemisphere as a naval surgeon, later writing extensively on the southern lands' floras, and then in the 1840s he received a grant to visit the Indian subcontinent. In 1865 he finally succeeded his father, Sir William Hooker, as director of Kew Gardens, with its by then magnificent herbarium.) Joseph Hooker married, on his return to England from India, Harriet Frances Henslow, daughter of the Reverend Professor John. Hooker was particularly interested in plant distributions, of vital interest to Darwin in the development of his evolutionary ideas. His long-time correspondent and beetle-collecting colleague from student days, cousin William Darwin Fox, was pressed for information on domestic animals and birds. The network of links established in his Cambridge days was utilized extensively. But so too was that other network that he had established during his shipboard days – but then the *Beagle* voyage had itself been a product of the Cambridge Network. He corresponded with Bartholomew Sulivan

(Lieutenant on the *Beagle*, who in the 1840s was stationed in the Falkland Islands) on a range of topics. These included the feral cattle, horses and pigs in the islands, fossils, the geology and topography of the archipelago, and the extent to which plant material was washed up on the Falklands' shores. All these fragments were grist to the mill of his mind as it ground out his evolutionary ideas. Information on domestic animals and the way in which they reverted when feral, and on long-distance dispersal, was particularly helpful. Through the late 1830s, the 1840s and the early 1850s, as his family was increasing and his garden was growing at Down House, Charles was building his edifice. He was in no hurry: he knew the opprobrium that those who rebelled against the Establishment brought on themselves. He also had his wife's religious susceptibilities to take into account. But there was a steadfastness of thought. Despite his affability, and sometimes diffident manner, he *knew* he was right. Despite the setbacks of illness, and the deaths of some of his children, he continued with his enquiries. Fairly early in the piece he tried out some of his ideas on Hensleigh Wedgwood and George Waterhouse. They were unimpressed. But Charles soldiered on.

He also, of course, read widely. He took a number of periodicals: one was the *Gardeners' Chronicle*, and in it Darwin took part in a correspondence about the viability of ancient seeds, and also on the role of bumble bees in the pollination of flowers. The seeds correspondence is interesting as it impinges on the long-distance dispersal phenomenon.

As was described in Chapter 11, by the middle of 1837, Darwin was a convinced transmutationist. Immense problems remained. Changes there seemed to have been, but how had they come about? An insight came from his reading. Towards the end of 1838 he picked up a copy of the sixth edition of Thomas Robert Malthus's (1766–1834) *Essay on Population*. The first edition had been published in 1798. It caused a stir.

Early in the essay (in fact a work of approaching 400 pages), he succinctly sets out the ideas for which he will be remembered, arguing from first principles:

> I think I may make two postulata. First, that food is necessary to the existence of man. Secondly, that passion between the sexes is necessary, and will remain nearly in

its present state ... Assuming then, my postulata as granted, I say, that the power of population is indefinitely greater than the power in the earth to produce subsistence for man. Population, when unchecked, increases in a geometrical ratio. Subsistence increases only in arithmetic ratio. A slight acquaintance with numbers will show the immensity of the first power in comparison with the second. By the law ... which makes food necessary, ... the effects of these two unequal powers must be kept equal. This implies a strong and constantly operating check on population from the difficulty of subsistence.

'Famine and pestilence,' he went on to argue, are the mechanisms that provide the 'check' to the otherwise inexorable growth in human numbers; in some of his writings he added war to this list. This pessimistic outlook was moderated in the second (1803) and later editions. Here the 'checks' were portrayed not as insuperable obstacles, but as defining limits; they were problems that had to be overcome if social progress were to be maintained. He did not *advocate* the spread of smallpox to control the rising population of the poor (as he was accused of doing), but he pointed out that hunger, poverty and disease went together, particularly with very large families. He *did* advocate what he called 'moral restraint', discouraging marriage, particularly early marriage (and therefore reproduction) among those who were unable to support themselves. He discouraged the distribution of food and money to the poor through relief programmes, maintaining that these simply caused the price of food to rise, and encouraged the poor to breed. To those who sided with the poor, Malthus was evil itself; to the middle classes who saw themselves as highly taxed he was a saviour.

Malthusian ideas were in wide circulation in fashionable (especially Whig) circles in London in the 1830s, around the time Charles Darwin returned from his voyage. Indeed Harriet Martineau (1802–76), the early feminist, and a strong propagandist for Malthusian ideas, was a girlfriend of Erasmus Darwin, Charles's elder brother, for a while. Charles indeed met Harriet Martineau at some of Erasmus's 'extravagant' dinner parties. Charles himself never met Malthus (he had died during the *Beagle* voyage), but the families had a number of acquaintances in common.

Malthusian doctrines provided Darwin with a key – a mechanism for the evolutionary process. Malthusian competition eliminated 'less favoured' individuals from the population, presenting their passing on their characteristics to later generations, and thus encouraging a progressive adaptation to environment. Darwin referred to this process as 'natural selection' and it became a critical component in the suite of his evolutionary ideas.

Darwin, throughout his career, was interested in the variations that occurred among domestic animals. He noted the striking similarity of all the individuals in a population of goats on an island off the coast of South America, and the way in which a feral population of cattle in the Falklands seemed to have reverted to an ancient, wilder form. Ensconced at Downe, he took an interest in the activities of local farmers and stock-breeders. In the 1850s he had a dovecote constructed at Down House, bought several pairs of fancy pigeons, and studied their breeding for himself. His daughter Etty (Henrietta) loved the birds. He also boiled, in a horrible chemical brew, the carcasses of both wild and domestic ducks to extract and compare their skeletons. Emma did not like the smell. At one stage, pondering the various intermediate stages between the fish-hunting otter of England's rivers and its probable land-dwelling ancestor, he wrote: 'Opponents will say, show me them. I will answer yes, if you will show me every step between the bulldog and greyhound.'

Islands had a fascination for Darwin from the *Beagle* days onwards. At one stage he asked Henslow why there were so many unique species on remote islands, although he thought he already knew the answer. If island biota were derived from mainland, continental environments, differentiating after arrival in their new home, the matter of long-distance dispersal was critical. Darwin did a number of experiments at Downe: he purchased some sea-salt and made up a solution approximately the same concentration as seawater and floated seeds of a variety of species in it for varying times. Some survived for substantial periods.

The study of animal behaviour was another theme that had interested Darwin from his days a-journeying onwards. In his *Beagle* notes he described the behaviour of many of the birds, mammals, reptiles and insects he encountered: bird calls and methods of locomotion, courtship, breeding, aggressive and feeding behaviour were recorded in detail. He noted the movements and changes in colour of octopuses in the Cape Verde Islands, and the response to light and other stimuli of planaria (flatworms) he collected in Tasmania. He quite early appreciated that these characteristics might have selection value and be inherited along with the morphology. He had witnessed the activities of the naked Fuegans in Tierra del Fuego. He could not avoid comparing their behaviour with that of the apes he spent hours watching at London Zoo. His notebooks contained many jottings on 'mind' and 'instinct'.

Gradually, over the years and decades, the picture came together. In the early summer of 1842, following a bout of ill health, he left London for several weeks and enjoyed the quiet seclusion of Maer and Shrewsbury. He was far enough along his trail to be able to draft a succinct summary of his ideas. It ran to 35 pages, and gives the impression of being written almost impulsively. There are no references; it is in pencil, on poor-quality paper; in places it lapses into what is almost note-form. The document has become known as the 'Sketch of 1842'. Commencing his account drawing attention to the phenomenon of variation in populations, he continues:

> When the organism is bred for several generations under new or varying conditions, the variation is greater in amount and endless in kind. ... The nature of the external conditions tends to effect some definite change in all or greater part of offspring. ... A certain degree of variation ... seems inevitable effect of process of reproduction.

He went on to emphasize how, through the ages, humanity has selected for certain characteristics in domestic animals and plants.

> By such selection make race-horse, dray-horse – one cow good for tallow, another for eating, etc. – one plant's good lay in leaves another in fruit ... [M]an selects only what is useful and curious.

'Let us see how far [the] above principles of variation apply to wild animals,' he continued. Wild creatures varied little, but were nevertheless individually distinguishable. Animals from different countries can be recognized as to their origin.

Our experience would lead us to believe that any and every one of these organisms would vary if the organism were taken away and placed under new conditions. Geology proclaims a constant round of changes, bringing into play, by every possible change of climate and the death of pre-existing inhabitants, endless variations of new conditions.

Animals and plants are adapted to their environment: plants with hooked seeds occur where there are 'woolly' animals; the woodpecker is adapted to crawl up trees; aquatic animals have webbed feet. Perhaps Nature, 'during thousands and thousands of years', selected 'all the variations which tended toward certain ends', rather in the way in which humans select for the characteristics in domestic animals and plants. He links the botanist de Candolle's notion of a 'war of nature' with the Malthusian idea of the existence of a check to expanding human population.

The unavoidable effect of this is that many of each species are destroyed … In the course of a thousand generations infinitesimal small differences must inevitably tell.

Long-legged hares would tend to survive the depredations of foxes; robins that survive 'years of destruction' – cold winters perhaps – would pass on their adaptations, just as breeders can produce monster-like transformation in pigeons. Darwin used the term 'natural selection' to describe this process for the first time.

Habits and the 'mental powers of different animals in wild and tame state … vary … and are inherited'. So too, possibly instincts. Relict organs, such as wings in flightless insects, cannot be explained by the theory of independent creation, but are readily accounted for by a theory of descent from some form that had full use of the organ. Nor can the similarities between great classes of organisms be explained except by reference to common descent. The bones of the wing of a bat, the hoof of a horse and the fin of a porpoise are remarkably similar, suggesting that they were all derived from the same common ancestor. '[A]ll mammals have descended from one stock,' he declaimed. The evidence from the geographical distribution of organisms is briefly reviewed, along with that from the fossil record, which he admits is incomplete.

Close to the conclusion of the 'Sketch' he wrote:

> From death, famine, rapine and the concealed war of nature we can see that the highest good, which we can conceive, the creation of the higher animals has directly come.

Darwin concludes with a remarkably well-crafted, almost mystical paragraph:

> There is a simple grandeur in the view of life with its powers of growth, assimilation and reproduction, being originally breathed into matter under one or a few forms, and that whilst this our planet has gone circling on according to fixed laws, and land and water, in a cycle of change, have gone on replacing each other, that from so simple an origin, through the process of gradual selection of infinitesimal changes, endless forms most beautiful and most wonderful have been evolved.

In January 1844 he wrote to Joseph Hooker that since he had returned from his voyage he had been 'engaged in a very presumptuous work', one which many would say was a very foolish one. He had been so impressed by the Galapagos organisms, and by the character of the South American mammal fossils, that he had been 'determined to collect ... every sort of fact, which cd bear in any way on what are species'.

> At last gleams of light have come, & I am almost convinced (quite contrary to the opinion I started with) that species are not (it is like confessing to murder) immutable. ... I think I have found out (here's presumption!) the simple way by which species become exquisitely adapted to various ends.

A fortnight later Hooker replied. In a long letter, mostly devoted to the distributions of southern hemisphere plants, he appended a note: 'There may in my opinion have been ... a gradual change of species. I shall be delighted to know how you think this change may have taken place.' He had obviously been thinking about the matter for he laconically added, 'no presently conceived opinions satisfy me on the subject'.

Darwin must have been gratified. His correspondence with Hooker became almost frenzied. Letters went back and forth in quick succession between Down and Kew (where Joseph Hooker was based, although he did not come into the directorship for many years). Their correspondence almost amounted to a collaboration: both benefited (another piece of good fortune). Not long after Hooker's acquiescence he commenced a much fuller expression of his evolutionary theories than the 1842 'Sketch'.

The 'Essay of 1844' was a much longer document – it ran to some 230 pages – and the style is much more polished. Some passages are virtually identical with the 'Sketch', for example the original concluding sentence beginning 'There is a grandeur in this view of life ...' (quoted above). Many of the same themes are taken up, but much greater detail is provided, and the notion of the transmutability of species is set out in full. Detailed examples are provided of the bearing of embryology, geographical distributions, affinities between organisms, the flora of remote islands, and very presciently 'the improbability of finding fossil forms intermediate between existing species', on his ideas. He goes into some detail on the 'principles of selection applicable to instincts'. The whole manuscript is a clear blueprint for his later work.

Darwin himself clearly attached enormous importance to the 'Essay'. On 5 July 1844 he wrote out a long letter to his wife, the opening sentences of which are as follows:

My Dear Emma,

I have just finished my sketch of my species theory. If, as I believe that my theory is true & it is accepted even by one competent judge, it will be a considerable step in science.

I therefore write this, in case of my sudden death, as my most solemn & last request, which I am sure you will consider the same as if legally entered in my will, that you will devote £400 to its publication, and further will yourself, or through Hensleigh [Wedgwood, Emma's brother], take trouble in promoting it.

There is more, including suggestions as to how this was to be accomplished. As well as the appropriate competent person receiving the modest honorarium, it was proposed that he receive all Darwin's natural history books that contained relevant material, scored or annotated by Darwin. Possible editors included Charles Lyell, Joseph Hooker, and, a little surprisingly, John Henslow. The notes on possible editorship were amended later. If all else failed, the 'Essay' was to be published as it was.

There were two sets of pressures on Darwin. There was the danger that he would be forestalled – that someone else would publish the same idea, and all Darwin's work would be wasted. There was also the possibility that if and when he did publish he would be vilified.

In 1844 a Scottish writer and publisher, Robert Chambers (1802–71), strongly influenced by Lamarck, wrote (and published anonymously) *Vestiges of the Natural History of Creation*, in part to open up the question of evolution to serious discussion. The book sold well: over 20,000 copies in a decade. US President Abraham Lincoln and Queen Victoria read it (the Queen strongly disapproved); so did poets such as Alfred Lord Tennyson and Elizabeth Barrett Browning, along with politicians like William Gladstone, and numerous scientists including Thomas Huxley and Adam Sedgwick.

Vestiges commenced with an explanation of the nebular hypothesis of the formation of the solar system, and went on to present a grand picture of the progressive evolution of life on earth. Chambers' real practical knowledge of science was quite limited, and he included much in his book that professional scientists found totally absurd. He accepted, and reported at some length, the experiments of an eccentric who claimed to have generated living mites (small, spider-like creatures) by passing electric currents through a chemical solution! Nevertheless he saw organic evolution as steady upward progress, governed by unknown, but ascertainable, natural laws. Some of those who knew about science ridiculed the book (Thomas Huxley was vicious in a review), although Darwin admitted it was well written and he must have felt a shiver of unease.

On the other hand, Charles Darwin did not wish to publish too early, with incomplete evidence or an ill-thought-out theory. He knew that there were many who would oppose an idea such as transmutation; he did not want their number to include competent scientists as well as conservative clerics. He confined his ideas to his family, and a few chosen colleagues. Charles Lyell, initially uncertain, was described by 1856 as 'coming round at a railway pace'. And where to publish? Submission of a paper to an academic journal would mean subjecting his material to editors and referees who might be critical, refuse to publish, and let the cat out of the bag. A book was perhaps more sensible.

So he plodded on, collecting information by reading and correspondence, by experiment and observation. The barnacle books (on which he had been working for over seven years) established his enhanced his reputation. He resolved, in about 1856, to write a monograph setting out his ideas and drafted many pages, much of it on plant distributions, with input from Hooker.

Experimentation continued. He fed some dead sparrows, their crops stuffed with oats, to an eagle at London Zoo: a few seeds germinated from pellets coughed up. So too with owl pellets. Perhaps this was a mechanism whereby plants could reach remote islands? Ideas half-formed while aboard the *Beagle* were put to the experimental test. In the Falklands he had wondered whether migrating birds might carry organisms from continental masses. Mud on the feet of ducks or geese might be a vehicle. From a 'tablespoonful' of mud from a pond he germinated 29 plants. The transportal of plants and animals to remote islands might be rare events, but it was quite possible, indeed entirely probable, when one took account of long stretches of geological time. His pigeons were also increasing in number and the variation within breeds provided a splendid analogy for changes with descent. His Big Species Book manuscript gradually swelled through the latter part of 1856, 1857 and early 1858. The title *Natural Selection* went through Darwin's mind.

But, as ever in life, three steps forward were followed by four backwards. His own health deteriorated once again. One of the doctors – a Dr Lane – who had treated him, and whom he liked, was accused of adultery and sensational reports of his trial appeared daily in the press. His daughter Henrietta was seriously ill with diphtheria, and other children were also poorly. Charles Waring, the backward, late addendum to the family, was a terrible source of worry; then he caught scarlet fever and on 29 June 1858 he died. Charles wrote to a friend at the time that he had had little but 'death & illness & misery' among his children. Into this hideous mess came the 'Bolt from the Blue'.

Alfred Russel Wallace was a social nobody. He was the son of an impoverished lawyer from the Welsh borderland. He left school at 14, and had trained as a land surveyor. He father had died when he was at a young age, and his elder brother, who had trained him, died in his twenties. He earned a living surveying the land parcelled out 'to the squires' following the passing of the Enclosure Acts: the enclosure of the common lands robbed the common people, he later opined. He learnt his botany and zoology in the woods, hedgerows and fields of Wales and, later, his socialism from evening institutes in London. He had picked up some vague evolutionary notions from *Vestiges*. Several of his attempts at money-earning failed and he resolved to try to earn a living collecting biological specimens and selling them to wealthy collectors. He set off for the Amazon with this in view, but on his return journey his ship burnt and the specimens were destroyed. Nevertheless, some of his scientific papers were making an impact, and he had corresponded with Darwin.

The 1850s found him in South East Asia, with a similar mixture of scientific and commercial objectives in view. Crates of specimens – bird skins, beetles, butterflies – were sent back to London for sale, but scientific enquiries (botanical, zoological and anthropological) were pursued with vigour between his bouts of fever. In February 1858 he wrote to Darwin enclosing (the original letter has not been found) a long manuscript with the title 'On the tendency of varieties to depart indefinitely from the original type'. The implication was that it should, if it was felt appropriate, be forwarded for publication in a scientific journal. Although there were differences of emphasis, the paper set out an evolutionary theory very similar to that of his own. Darwin was mortified: his originality was 'smashed'. It was almost as though Wallace had a copy of the 1844 'Essay' before him, he complained. Lyell had foreseen this, counselling his friend against delay, but it was hard to bear. Bad luck piled upon bad luck; misfortune on misfortune. Because of all his other troubles Darwin found it difficult to focus.

Lyell and Hooker took matters in hand. Darwin and Wallace would announce their findings together; neither could be accused of attempting to forestall the other; Darwin would not be accused of holding back material sent to him in good faith, or of stealing his priority.

A meeting of the Linnean Society was scheduled for Thursday 1 July 1858: the last before the summer break; it had, fortunately for Darwin, been postponed when Society member David Brown died. With considerable sleight of hand at what was almost literally the eleventh hour, Joseph Hooker and Charles Lyell inserted the cobbled together Darwin–Wallace presentation into the agenda. It consisted of extracts from the 'Essay', and from a letter he had written to his American correspondent (and eventual firm supporter), Asa Gray at Harvard, together with Wallace's paper. Hooker and Lyell introduced the documents with a letter:

> The accompanying papers, which we have the honour of communicating to the Linnean Society, and which are all on the same subject, viz the Laws which affect the Production of Varieties, Races, and Species contain the results of the investigations of two indefatigable naturalists, Mr Charles Darwin and Mr Alfred Wallace.

The letter went on to explain how these two, 'independently and unknown to one another', had developed 'the same very ingenious theory'. In a little twist to highlight their friend's priority, they gave the three papers 'in the order of their dates'.

About 30 fellows were present, and the presentation was squeezed in among several other papers, all rather rushed. Probably many of those present did not understand what they were hearing. The term damp squib has been used to describe the event. Then, as at other meetings where his work was discussed, Charles absented himself; he was burying his poor baby son, and comforting his wife in the churchyard at Downe. His misery and misfortune continued: just over a fortnight later his sister Marianne died, aged 60, leaving a large family.

But the theory was at last in the public domain. The papers were published in the Linnean Society journal, and within months some naturalists were using the ideas. Months later, when in October 1858 he heard from Hooker what had been done, Wallace was extremely pleased, and expressed his gratitude to Darwin, Hooker and Lyell. Even Darwin came to realize that the 'Bolt from the Blue' might have been a blessing in disguise. Were it not for Wallace's letter the publication of the great theory might have remained under wraps for further years. Good fortune came out of bad, once again.

But Darwin could not afford to let the grass grow. Darwin had his incomplete *Natural Selection* manuscript dominating his life. Big Species Book indeed – it ran to over a quarter of a million words. Who would publish such a Leviathan? He decided that the most sensible course of action was to publish an 'Abstract' of this massive work, as quickly as possible, and with a minimum of references and 'scholarly apparatus'. The full *Natural Selection* manuscript itself languished for well over a century, until Cambridge University Press took the plunge in 1975.

There were further family distractions, and other work, including helping Hooker with his book on the Flora of Australia, and writing a quite lengthy paper on the fertilization of leguminous plant flowers by bees. He was also struggling with further ill health and wrote to his son William on 15 October that his 'stomach has been horridly bad'. Despite these inconveniences, by Christmas Eve 1858 he had 'written 330 folio pages' of his abstract but expected it would 'require 150–200'. Nevertheless, his letters show that he was still seeking out information. Work went on, as fast as Darwin's erratic health would allow, into the New Year. By April the 'Big Book' had been compressed to a little over half its original length. Reliable, ever-positive Charles Lyell acted as midwife and persuaded John Murray, a well-known London publisher, to accept it unseen. Darwin struggled with depression, anxiety and sickness through the summer, as he corrected the proofs, to publisher Murray's chagrin, revising heavily as he went. The bill for corrections was high, but was picked up by Murray.

The 'Abstract' was published on 24 November 1859 as *On the Origin of Species by Means of Natural Selection, or the Preservation of Favoured Races in the Struggle for Life*. In it, Darwin develops 'one long argument', with numerous empirical examples as support, for his theory that 'groups' (populations) of animals and plants, rather than individual organisms, gradually evolve or change, throughout time, through the process of natural selection.

The book is remarkably readable, written in a very clear rhetorical style, even if some of the sentences are rather long, and the style somewhat quaint to the modern ear. The book attracted widespread interest on publication. Despite the relatively high price of 15 shillings, the printing of 1,250 copies sold out at once. The second edition appeared six weeks later, in January 1860. Perhaps to assuage religious susceptibilities (his wife Emma was very religious) the words, 'by the Creator' were inserted into the famous closing sentence of the book, so that it read:

> There is grandeur in this view of life, with its several powers, having been originally breathed by the Creator into a few forms or into one; and that, whilst this planet has gone circling on according to the fixed law of gravity, from so simple a beginning endless forms most beautiful and most wonderful have been, and are being evolved.

Darwin's approach has been described as rhetorical as he attempts to present an argument, supported by evidence, then suggests possible objections, in due course answering them. Almost every chapter ends with a concise summary, so that the reader can assess the argument as it develops, and prepare himself for the next step.

The structure is extremely logical, and conceived so as to persuade. Darwin starts from the familiar: Chapter 1 is entitled 'Variation under domestication', as everyone can be expected to be familiar with the various breeds of domestic animals and farm and garden plants. The varieties of Darwin's beloved pigeons are taken as a particular case study. In Chapter 2 Darwin extends the discussion to 'Variation under nature'. In Chapter 3 the concept of competition, or as he puts in the first edition, 'the struggle for life', is introduced, and the Malthusian doctrines of geometrical increase and the 'checks' on increases are discussed. Chapter 4 leads into 'Natural selection', comparing it to selection by humans, and shows how it may work 'on characters of trifling importance' over time. Chapter 5 is headed 'Laws of Variation', and links the idea of inheritance to natural selection; working before the science of genetics was developed, Darwin's treatment was necessarily incomplete.

Having set up his 'theory of descent with modification', Chapter 6 addresses the 'Difficulties of the theory', in particular the absence or rarity of transitional varieties. Chapter 7 is directed towards 'Instinct'; here Darwin claims that similar generalizations in terms of variation, competition and inheritance apply to animals' instincts and the habits of animals as can be applied to their physical form. He provides a wide range of examples:

parasitism in the cuckoo and in other organisms; the taking of slaves by some species of ants; the cell-making instinct in hive-bees.

The next group of chapters seeks to bolster up his arguments with evidence from particular sources. Chapter 8 discusses 'Hybridism' and the sterility of some hybrids.

Chapter 9 again raises the possibility of 'difficulties', headed as it is 'On the imperfection of the geological record': the rarity of intermediate forms in the fossil record, as well as among living organisms is acknowledged, and attempts are made to explain it in terms of the 'intermittence' of geological formations, and the poverty of fossil collections that existed at the time. Nevertheless, in Chapter 10 – 'On the geological succession of organic beings' – he attempts to show, to some extent at least, how palaeontology supports his theories. Two chapters on 'Geographical Distribution' (11 and 12) then follow; these show how the distribution of organisms, particularly the occurrence and non-occurrence of certain biological groups on islands, supports the theory of evolution. In Chapter 13 the supporting evidence of the affinities between biological groups, embryology and the presence of rudimentary organs is marshalled. Classification of plants and animals, Darwin argues, should be based on their evolutionary relationship. The final chapter (14) is headed 'Recapitulation and Conclusion'; after again reviewing 'the difficulties on the theory of natural selection', he summarizes the evidence in favour, and briefly, mentions some of its implications. The book is indeed 'one long argument': logically structured and carefully crafted. Despite delays, family misfortunes, near forestalment, periods of ill health, and family tragedies, determination had been rewarded. The Squire of Downe had reached his destination.

23. Charles Darwin in middle life. From an early edition of Darwin's works.

13

Afterwards

Darwin published *On the Origin* when he was 50, and in many ways this represented a high point of his life. But he lived another 23 years. He was anxious to the point of illness about the possible reception of his work in the months leading up to publication. In some ways his predictions proved all too accurate.

Fairly late in his life Darwin received the following, sent anonymously:

> The learned Darwin states that Moses taught confusion
> For Man, he boldly states, descends from Ape or Monkey.
> I, having read his book, come to this conclusion –
> Darwin (at least himself) descends from Ass or Donkey!

There would have been many, in the nineteenth century, in the conventional English, Anglican, establishment, and among the more conservative Christians in many countries, particularly the USA, who would have agreed completely with this master of doggerel. But there were many who would not.

In the medieval period, and indeed until well into the sixteenth century, the notion that the Book of Genesis contained the literal truth concerning the origin of the universe, of the earth and of life was widespread: there was general agreement that the world had been created in six days, and that this had happened not more than a very few thousand years ago. James Ussher (1581–1656), Bishop of Meath and later Archbishop of Armagh (in Ireland), wrote *Annales veteris et novis testamenti* (Annals of the Old and New Testaments) (1650–4), stating that the date of Creation was 4004 BC; the date and time of day were also specified. Bishop Ussher's chronology was widely accepted and was printed in some Bibles from 1701 onwards, although it was never official Anglican doctrine; other dates were also supported by some scholars. Some early geologists saw their task as one of reconciliation – the reconciling of the 'Book of Moses' with the 'Book of the Rocks'. The term 'scriptural geologists' is sometimes applied to such persons.

By the middle of the nineteenth century, however, most geologists, particularly after the publication of Charles Lyell's *Principles of Geology* (1831–3), were convinced of the 'old earth' hypothesis – the idea that the world was much older than the likes of Bishop Ussher asserted, and was possibly millions of years old. Sometimes interesting intellectual gymnastics were performed by those who accepted a longer earth history, but still wished to 'reconcile'. Some suggested that the six days of the Genesis Creation were very 'long days' – that they represented six extended periods of time rather than six modern days of 24 hours. Others supported the idea that there was a long period between the initial Creation and the six days specified in Genesis. The 'literalist' interpretation of the book of Genesis as providing an accurate account of the origin of the earth and of life upon it was already crumbling by the time *On the Origin* appeared.

In fact there was a wide variation in the way in which Darwin's views were received. Certainly Professor Adam Sedgwick, vice-master of Trinity College, Cambridge, and Canon of Norwich Cathedral, when he was training the young Darwin in geological field techniques in North Wales in the summer of 1831, would not have attached a great deal of importance to James Ussher's computations: devout Christian he may have been, but he was certainly not an extreme literalist. Yet after reading *On the Origin* for the first time in November 1859, he wrote the famous 'kind yet slashing letter' to his former protégé, including the words:

> I call (in the abstract) causation the will of God: & I can prove He acts for the good of all His creatures. He also acts by laws which we can study & comprehend. … We all admit development as a fact of history: but how came it about? …

Sedgwick seems to broadly accept Darwin's idea of change over time

– development – but argues more about mechanism. Sedgwick is here within the William Paley, Natural Theology tradition that sees the diversity, beauty and complexity of the natural world as evidence of the creative power of God, and the adaptation of organisms to their environment as evidence that 'He acts for the good of all His creatures'.

The Yorkshire parson-ornithologist, Francis Orpen Morris (1810–93) provides an example of a much more trenchant, almost vicious, critic. He attacked Darwin's theories in pamphlets (such as *Difficulties with Darwinism* (1869), and *The Demands of Darwinism on Credulity* (1890)), in sermons, and in speeches for 25 years, seeing it as his life's work to discredit the 'monstrous puerilites' expressed in Darwin's books. How could organisms change over time and yet inherit characters from their parents?

Richard Owen (1804–92) was much closer to the centre of scientific power. From his throne of superintendent of the natural history collections at the British Museum he was able to exert more influence than a slightly eccentric, somewhat bigoted Yorkshire clergyman. He wrote what Darwin described as a clever but spiteful, malignant and damaging review of the *Origin* in the April 1860 *Edinburgh Review*. Indeed he accused Darwin of erecting a straw man. Transmutation was nonsense. Owen was not a biblical traditionalist, but he believed that new species, throughout geological time, had entered the world at a stroke: 'the ordained becoming of living things'.

Thomas Huxley in the *Westminster Review* answered with a vengeance. He castigated Owen. 'Darwinism' gave scientists a flag under which they could march, he propounded, and would allow Science to influence 'regions of thought where she has, as yet, hardly penetrated'. Continuing the military metaphor (he had served in the Royal Navy), he asserted that *On the Origin* provided a 'Whitworth gun in the armoury of liberalism'.

The arguments ricocheted across the Atlantic. The interest that the book had generated in Britain encouraged several US publishers to issue pirate editions there. (There was no network of international copyright agreements, as there is now.) Harvard botanist Asa Gray (1810–88), who had been within Darwin's chosen circle quite early and who had been the original recipient of a letter put in as part of the Linnean Society presentation, took up the

24. The Reverend Francis Orpen Morris, one of Darwin's acerbic critics. From a nineteenth century print.

cudgels on Darwin's behalf. He discouraged two of the publishers, and negotiated a royalty-paying agreement with the third. Although he did not agree with every aspect of Darwin's theory, he made it his business to see that his work was received fairly. His own review of the *Origin* was by far the most competent to appear in the USA. His *Free Examination of Darwin's Treatise on the Origin of Species* appeared in 1861, and other generally supportive works followed. These acted as important publicity for Darwin's notions on that side of the Atlantic.

While Huxley became known as 'Darwin's bulldog', Gray has been called 'Darwin's retriever', in that he rescued or retrieved Darwin's thought for Christians. He saw *On the Origin* as a continuation of Paleyan natural theology; natural selection did not exclude the possibility of design. On the other hand, the Princeton theologian, Charles Hodge (1797–1878), an evangelical Presbyterian, mounted a multi-pronged assault on Darwin and Darwinism that went on for years. In *Systematic Theology* he claimed that Darwin's ideas were atheistic:

> Mr. Darwin and his associates ... admit ... only the creation of matter, but of living matter, in the form of one or a few primordial germs from which without any purpose or design, by the slow operation of unintelligent natural causes, and accidental variations, during untold ages, all the orders, classes, genera, species, and varieties of plants and animals, from the lowest to the highest, man included, have been formed. Teleology, and therefore, mind, or God, is expressly banished from the world. (*Systematic Theology*, volume 2 (1873), page 23)

First of all, it is an assault upon common sense, Hodge claimed, to be told that 'the whale and the humming-bird, man and the mosquito' are derived from the same source. Second, the theory cannot be correct as it is based on an impossible assumption: that 'matter does the work of mind'. Hodge argues design in the Paleyan manner. His objection is that Darwin argues against the intervention of mind (a designer) anywhere in the process and that this is incredible. Third (an extension of the second point), 'the system is thoroughly atheistic and therefore cannot possibly stand'. Darwin asserts that God has had nothing to do with the universe since the creation of one or more 'living germ' or 'germs', and to Hodge, this is tantamount to atheism.

Hodge's fourth remark is that the theory is a mere hypothesis, and incapable of proof by its very nature. Hodge's works were (and to some extent still are) influential, especially in the USA.

On the other hand, many naturalists saw no conflict between their Christian faith and Darwin's ideas. Charles Kingsley (1819–75), Rector of Eversley, in Hampshire – naturalist, novelist, social activist, polymath – was an enthusiastic supporter from his first reading of *On the Origin*. On receiving the book, he wrote to Darwin, 'All I have seen awes me' and 'I shall prize your book'. After agreeing with Darwin's argument that species are impermanent, he concluded 'that it is just as noble a conception of the Deity' to believe that original forms were created that could develop and change as to maintain that new forms had to be created to fill the gaps that 'he himself had made'.

Later in an address he declaimed:

> And if it be said that the doctrine of evolution, by doing away with the theory of creation, does away with that of final causes – let us answer boldly – Not in the least. We might accept what Mr Darwin and Professor Huxley have written on physical science, and yet preserve our natural theology on exactly the same basis as that on which Butler and Paley left it. That we should develop it, I do not deny. That we should relinquish it, I do. (F. Kingsley, *Life and Memories*, 1877, p. 347)

Charles Kingsley was an important influence in determining the reception of Darwin's ideas by the British Establishment, and by clergy in the Church of England. Perhaps partly as the result of his influence there were many clergy, in the Church of England, and to some extent in other denominations, who came to take a similar view (Roman Catholics excepted, until well into the twentieth century). Some found Darwin's ideas liberating: it was no longer necessary to believe that the creation stories in Genesis were the 'complete literal truth', although they might have value. By the nineteenth century, biblical scholars were pointing out discrepancies and differences within the scriptural texts. Parts of Genesis and other sections of the Old Testament were myths, or allegories, containing important truths and ideas, maybe, but impossible to regard as accurate scientifically. The Victorian era was also the heyday of the parson-naturalist. There were many English clergy, trained in the Natural Theology tradition, who saw the study of the living world as a logical extension of their work as priests. Such men believed that by exploring the complexity and beauty of the living world in their studies of seaweeds, spiders or sponges, liverworts, leeches or lichens, they were gaining an insight into the mind of the Creator. Many of them began to use Darwin's theories in this work.

Charles Lyell and Joseph Hooker, of course, responsible for introducing the theory of the transmutability of species as the result of natural selection to the scientific community that summer evening in 1858, were dogged supporters and publicists (although Lyell had reservations where it came to the evolution of humans).

Another early Darwinian disciple was Thomas Huxley (1825–95), former naval surgeon and for a time professor at the School of Mines. He was initially an opponent of evolutionary ideas, taking particular exception to the directionality, or teleological nature (i.e. the idea that evolution represented 'progress', or movement towards a goal) in the evolutionary theories of Lamarck and Chambers. However, when he first read *On the Origin of Species* he is said to have remarked, 'How stupid of me not to have thought of that!'

His letter to Darwin (dated 23 November 1859) on his first reading of the book is of considerable interest:

My dear Darwin

I finished your book yesterday ... no work on Natural History Science I have met with has made so great an impression upon me & I do most heartily thank you for the great store of new views you have given me.

Nothing ... can be better than the tone of the book – it impresses those who know nothing about the subject. As for your doctrines, I am prepared to go to the Stake if requisite in support ...

I trust you will not allow yourself to be in any way disgusted or annoyed by the considerable abuse & misrepresentation which unless I greatly mistake is in store for you. Depend on it you have earned the lasting gratitude of all thoughtful men. And as to the curs which will bark & yelp, you must recollect that some of your friends … are endowed with an amount of combativeness … which may stand you in good stead.

Huxley did not accept every aspect of the theory. It the same letter he said that 'You have loaded yourself with an unnecessary difficulty in adopting *Natura non facit saltum* [nature does not make leaps] so unreservedly. I believe she does make small jumps.'

Despite his reservations, Thomas Huxley became one of Darwin's most staunch defenders – hence the nickname 'Darwin's bulldog'. Perhaps Huxley is best known for his role in championing the evolutionary point of view in the 'Great Debate' at the Oxford meeting of the British Association for the Advancement of Science in June 1860, held under the chairmanship (by all accounts very fair and impartial) of Professor John Henslow. Huxley's opponent in the debate was Samuel Wilberforce, Bishop of Oxford. During the debate (which Darwin did not attend), Wilberforce, who, although he had some knowledge of science, had been coached by Richard Owen, ridiculed the concept of evolution. Accounts of the debate vary a good deal, but the Bishop is said to have asked Huxley whether he would prefer to be descended from an ape on his grandfather's or grandmother's side. In a letter written by Huxley himself some time later he stated that his reply was:

> If … the question is put to me would I rather have a miserable ape for a grandfather or a man highly endowed by nature and possessed of great means of influence & yet who employs these faculties for the mere purpose of introducing ridicule into a grave scientific discussion – I unhesitating affirm my preference for the ape. (T. H. Huxley to Frederick Daniel Dyster, written about September 1860)

Joseph Hooker (who also spoke vigorously) and other Darwin friends and supporters proclaimed Huxley the winner of the debate, but some less partisan people in the audience, estimated at 700 to 1,000, asserted that it was more evenly balanced.

Perhaps Huxley's most notable book was *Evidence as to Man's Place in Nature*, published in 1863 – five years after *On the Origin*, in which Darwin had said nothing on human evolution, stating only, at the end of the book, that eventually 'light will be thrown on the origin of Man'. Huxley's *Evidence* attempted to review what was known of primate and human anatomy, palaeontology and behaviour. This was the first book to deal systematically with the topic of human evolution.

Again this caused a confrontation with Richard Owen. Owen claimed that the human brain contained parts that were not present in the brains of apes, and thus humans could not possibly be descended from apes. Huxley showed that the brains of apes and humans were fundamentally very similar. Huxley was a belligerent opponent, and positively hated Owen. Owen reciprocated. When Huxley was elected to the Council of the Zoological Society, Owen resigned. In 1862 Huxley intervened to prevent Owen being elected to the Council of the Royal Society, accusing him of uttering 'deliberate falsehoods'.

Huxley's pugnacious style was anathema to older, gentlemen naturalists, but he was unrepentant. And his well-orchestrated campaign, with the support of the likes of Lyell and Hooker, and Asa Gray across the ocean, resulted in the Darwinians, in less than a decade, having triumphed, at least in the scientific community. The discovery of *Archaeopteryx*, a fossil apparently intermediate between a reptile and a bird, in Germany in 1861 gratified Darwin: in *On the Origin* he accepted that intermediates between forms were rare in the fossil record, but predicted they would be found. The timing was perfect (Darwin's luck again?). The specimen was bought by the British Museum at great expense. A description appeared in 1863. So by 1866 it could be said that the battle was won. In that year Darwin's ideas dominated the Nottingham meeting of the British Association for the Advancement of Science. One commentator claimed that Darwinism was 'everywhere in the ascendant'. In every section of the Association's meeting Darwin's views on descent had 'leavened the scientific mind'. One could say that in the ecosystem of the world of ideas, theories that had a competitive advantage, that had some utility, had become dominant over older, more primitive notions, less able to advance science.

Darwin had missed the Linnean Society presentation. He had missed the 'Great Debate' in Oxford. Some people commented that without his team of defenders the story might have been different. He had been advised to take six months' rest after the publication of *On the Origin*. What he got was rather more than six months' sickness; perpetual tiredness and weakness, vomiting and headaches laid him low for weeks at a time. He was worried about his children too: ideas about the deleterious effects of cousin marriages haunted him. Three children had died. Two of his sisters had also passed away within a year. His son Leonard was thought to be 'slow and backward' and required special tutoring. Henrietta was very weak and feverish for years on end and required round the clock nursing. They all gave rise to anxiety of one sort or another.

But Darwin's indomitable spirit triumphed over these misfortunes. Large parts of the Big Species Book had been hastily stripped away to produce the manageable 'Abstract' – *On the Origin*. Economical in many things, Darwin recycled some of it in a series of books published, almost at the rate of one a year, after 1868. Letters continued to come and go as they had done throughout his career as he sought information from colleagues all over the world. He was still doing experiments, for example on pollination mechanisms of flowers, and the inheritance of characteristics in poultry and pigeons. Trips for his own health or that of his children to different parts of the country – he never went abroad again after his return from the *Beagle* – allowed him to encounter different environments, and see different species of plants and animals: insect-trapping sundews in Sussex; insect-pollinated orchids in Devon. Darwin was always as interested in the relationships between organisms as in the organisms themselves. The relationship between humans and domestic animals and plants had fascinated him since his sojourn on the *Beagle*. The first chapter of *On the Origin of Species* had been titled 'Variation under domestication' and commenced as follows:

> When we look to the individuals of the same variety or sub-variety of our older cultivated plants and animals, one of the first points that strikes us, is, that they generally differ much more from each other, than do individuals of any one species or variety in a state of nature.

The artificial selection of particular traits by farmer, stock-breeder and gardener, from the natural variation of plants and animals, Darwin argued, was responsible for the great diversity of breeds domesticated or cultivated by humans. The final sentence in Chapter 1 of the *Origin* was:

> I am convinced that the accumulative action of Selection, whether applied methodically and more quickly, or unconsciously and more slowly, but more efficiently is by far the predominant Power.

From 'Variation under domestication' Darwin had gone on to 'Variation under nature' in Chapter 2, and then on to the 'Struggle for existence' and to 'Natural selection'. His consideration of the variability of domestic plants and animals is thus the important first element in his 'long argument' set out in the book as a whole.

Charles Darwin expanded his ideas on domestic organisms in his book the *Variation of Animals and Plants under Domestication*, published in 1868. In this work he expressed his intention to:

> … give under the head of each species only the facts I have been able to collect or observe, showing the amount and nature of the changes which animals and plants have gone undergone whilst under man's dominion, or which bear on the general principles of variation. (*Variation of Animals and Plants under Domestication*, 1868, Chapter 1)

In *Variation of Animals and Plants* he considered cats, dogs, pigs, horses, asses, cattle, sheep, goats, rabbits, chickens, ducks, geese, peacocks, turkeys, guinea-fowl, goldfish, hive-bees and guinea fowl, although his most detailed case study was of pigeons, firmly based on his own observations and research. Cereals and vegetables are also considered. The purpose of the book (which went into several editions) is to show how the range of normal variation is acted on by deliberate selection by humans, and the 'accidental' selection pressures of the field and farmyard, to produce the diversity of breeds and strains that exist today. It thus served to drive home one of the main points on which he had based the argument in *On the Origin of Species*.

Darwin said little concerning the evolution of humans in *On the Origin*, although the derivation of humans from an ape-like ancestor was implicit, a point that lubricated the Great Debate and other intellectual battles of the day. Canny Darwin thought that to labour this point too strongly might be to take things too far at that stage. Huxley had no such scruples and lectured and wrote frequently on the perceived close relationship between humans and apes, his studies culminating in his book on *Man's Place in Nature* in 1863. At around the same time, in February 1863, Charles Lyell followed with the *Antiquity of Man*, which demonstrated that humans had existed for a long period, and that primitive stone tools had been found in the same cave deposits as extinct animals. But in Lyell's book the link to the ape was fudged. Darwin despaired of his close friend.

But both *Antiquity* and *Place* had prepared the ground, and the time was right for Darwin to take the bull by the horns.

The full title of the work in question is *The Descent of Man and Selection in Relation to Sex*. This emphasizes that the book is divided into two parts – in reality two rather separate books, which in the first (1871: a few copies bear an 1870 date) edition appeared as two discrete volumes. In subsequent editions they were united. As in *On the Origin*, he provided an enormous array of facts, carefully arranged to support his strong arguments.

In his Introduction to the book Darwin announces:

> The sole object of this work is to consider, firstly, whether man, like every other species, is descended from some pre-existing form; secondly, the manner of his development; and thirdly, the value of the differences between the so-called races of man. (*Descent of Man*, Introduction, 2nd edition)

The book is also of great significance as the word 'evolution' appears on page 2 (i.e. in the Introduction) of the first volume of the first edition. This is the first time this word appears in any of Charles Darwin's works: this anticipates its use in the sixth edition of *On the Origin*. (The verb 'evolves' appears earlier.)

Chapter 1 rehearses the evidence for the descent of modern man from some lower form. It describes the homologous (similar in form) structures, notes similarities in habits and behaviour, and comments on similarities in the diseases that affect humans and other animals, particularly the great apes and monkeys. He also notes the striking similarities in the range of parasites that infect them. The similarity of the embryonic forms of humans and other mammals is noted, along with the presence of rudimentary organs: it is argued for example that the thin layer of hairs on the body of most humans is a relic of the thick coat of hair or fur on the bodies of other mammals.

Chapter 2 is headed 'Manner of development', and applies the concepts set out in *On the Origin* to humans – examples of variation, competition and 'the struggle for existence' are given. Chapters 3 and 4 compare the mental powers of humans and the lower animals, and Chapter 5 speculates on the possibility of 'the advancement of intellectual powers through natural selection'. The final two chapters of Part 1 discuss the various races of humanity, and their formation, differentiation, and affinities – in other words they seek to apply evolutionary ideas to the various members of the human family.

The second part of the book is devoted to sexual selection. Darwin realized that the principle of natural selection was responsible for the differences between the sexes in animals. Usually (but far from universally) it is the male that is more flamboyant in colouration, or has the more elaborate secondary sexual characteristics. Male stag beetles have massive 'claws' or mandibles, peacocks have their striking tails, stags (male deer) have sometimes enormous antlers, male butterflies are often much more brightly coloured than the female. Male humans have beards and hairy chests (Darwin himself provided a fine example of the former in later life!). He suggests that these adornments convey a selective advantage: a female was more likely to mate with the male that had the more spectacular adornment, the antlers that led to victory in conflict, or a more striking courtship display. Sexual selection thus provided a special case of natural selection.

The reception of the *Descent* was perhaps marginally less controversial than that of *On the Origin*. Nevertheless, in the preface to the second edition (1874) he mentions the 'fiery ordeal through which this book has passed'. The clamour following the *Origin* had died down, and the notion of transmutability of species had been accepted by many, but the specific assertion that humans were descended from ape-like ancestors still transgressed some Victorian mores.

Much of Charles Darwin's time in his later years was taken up with the constant revision of his earlier books for new editions. *On the Origin* went into a second printing within weeks of its first appearing. Six editions appeared in his lifetime, and the later ones underwent extensive revision. For example, many scientists were concerned about the chance or 'higgledy-piggledy' nature of the selection mechanism. Moreover, physicists were speculating that the earth might be only 100 million years old, or even less (using the rate of heat loss from the inner earth, assuming a 'hot' origin for the earth). If there were a very low rate for the generation of beneficial variations this would appear far too short for the diversity of living forms now on earth to evolve. In the fifth edition of *On the Origin* Darwin, perhaps unfortunately, modified his text to take account of this, suggesting that the environment might accelerate the rate at which variations occurred, and thus accelerate the rate of evolution. Moreover he resurrected the rather Lamarckian idea of 'use-inheritance'. The continued use of an organ caused its growth, he claimed, and these changes could be inherited.

As well as continuing attacks on his theories – and although their ferocity declined, each new edition of *On the Origin* or the *Descent of Man* brought more – there were problems at home. His dear daughter Henrietta, who had walked around the Sandwalk and nurtured the pigeons with him, and helped him with tasks such as correcting proofs, married, in 1871, someone who was harmless enough (he was musical, worked for the Ecclesiastical Commissioners, and lectured at a Working Men's College). But to some he appeared a bit of a fop. Charles could tolerate Richard Litchfield – 'a stout, shortsighted barrister' with a 'sweet smile' – but could hardly bear losing his Etty. William was working in a bank in Southampton, Frank was studying medicine, and George was reading for the Bar. Leonard was going into the Royal Engineers and Horace was at Cambridge. And although the house often seemed empty, Charles should have been proud of his brood. But worry pursued him wherever he went. The health of all of them was poor – or at least that was what he, and perhaps they, felt. They frequently came home, allegedly unwell, to be nursed by Emma. And he was always ill himself. His stomach continually gave him trouble, and his head …. Sometimes, for months on end he could only do a few hours' work a day.

But the work went on. Since shortly after returning from the sea, Darwin had maintained notebooks dealing with aspects of animal behaviour, human emotions and aspects of 'Mind'. Perhaps changes in mental attributes had accompanied or even preceded changes in appearance and morphology. While on the *Beagle*, jottings on the behaviour of animals had been recorded alongside their descriptions. A baby diary had recorded the early months of his youngest son's life. Richard Owen's criticisms of his work, and that of Thomas Huxley, included comments that, whatever their superficial similarity, there were fundamental differences between humans and the apes. Darwin noted the fundamental similarity between the muscles of the human face and those of apes – there were also, he thought, similarities in the way these were used to express emotion. Years before he had watched apes at the London Zoo, thinking of similarities to the Fuegans. Some of these themes were brought together in his *Expression of Emotions in Man and Animals*, published in 1872, which represented the third stage (after *On the Origin* and *Descent of Man*) in Darwin's campaign to demonstrate that humans have evolved from other species of animals. Many of our emotions and mental abilities can be seen in humanity's remote ancestors, he argued. The book provides an important part of the basis of modern psychology and ethology (the study of animal behaviour).

The penultimate paragraph in the book reads:

> We have seen that the study of the theory of expression confirms to a certain limited extent the conclusion that man is derived from some lower animal form, and supports the belief of the specific or sub-specific unity of the several races; but as far as my judgment serves, such confirmation was hardly needed. (*Expression of Emotions*, Chapter 14)

Some might say that Darwin pushes his argument too far. In stressing the essential unity of animal life, and the common origins of humans and animals, he becomes somewhat anthropomorphic, attributing to animals distinctly human emotions and values, as for example when he describes the 'love' that a bitch has for her puppies, or the manner in which a dog licks the body of a cat with which it is 'friends'. But Darwin was working in his own time, with the vocabulary available to him. His organization of a tremendous wealth of observed detail around broad themes, and effectively laying the foundations of a whole new subject, are impressive achievements.

Domestication carried the first chapter of the *Origin* forward, developing a wealth of examples. *Descent* and *Emotions* developed the whole notion of humanity's origins. But there is another branch of the tree – a botanical branch. This constituted a separate enterprise. The *Fertilisation of Orchids* appeared in 1862, *On the Movements and Habits of Climbing Plants* in 1865, and *Insectivorous Plants* in 1875. Three even more specialized botanical works also appeared towards the end of his life: *The Effects of Cross and Self Fertilisation in the Vegetable Kingdom* (1876), which explored similar themes to the Orchids volume, the *Different Forms of Flowers of the Same Species* (1877) and *The Power of Movement in Plants* (1880), which addresses similar issues to *Climbing Plants* (sales of these last three were small). The contents of some of these botanical volumes had been previously published. They are the result of painstaking experimental work in his greenhouses and his continuing correspondence with his botanist colleagues such as Asa Grey and Joseph Hooker. All these have evolutionary themes, although the message is perhaps slightly less overt than in *On the Origin*, *Domestication* or *Descent*.

The first book published in this botanical stream was entitled *On the Various Contrivances by which Orchids are Fertilised by Insects* (usually abbreviated to *Fertilisation of Orchids*). It was first published in 1862, just two years after *On the Origin* (a second edition appeared in 1877). The work stresses the themes of adaptation to environment, the relationships between organisms, and the importance of cross-fertilization as a source of variation. Although these are ideas that are expounded in the *Origin*, Darwin's American friend, botanist Asa Gray, wrote: '[I]f the Orchid-book (with a few trifling omissions) had appeared before the *Origin*, the author would have been canonised rather than anathematised by the natural theologians' school.' Gray also described it as a flanking movement in the battle for the acceptance of the notion of evolution through natural selection. Indeed, one periodical, the *Literary Churchman*, in an otherwise favourable review, declaimed that 'Darwin's expression of admiration at the contrivances in orchids is too indirect a way of saying, "O Lord, how manifold are Thy works"'. A good deal of Darwin's work has been seen as just one step away from William Paley's *Natural Theology*.

The orchids book shows, in great detail, the relationships between the structure of orchid blooms and the insects that pollinate them, their development being explained by natural selection. Darwin argued that while many orchids (and indeed other flowers) were hermaphroditic – the flowers had both male and female sexual organs – it was advantageous for crossing to occur. This, he believed, would promote variation (the basis of natural selection) and 'vitality'. Insects moved from one bloom to another in their search for nectar, fertilizing one flower with pollen from another, and so mechanisms ('contrivances') that encouraged cross-pollination had survival value, and thus would tend to be 'favoured'. He summarized the situation:

> In my examination of Orchids, hardly any fact has struck me so much as the endless diversity of structures … for gaining the very same end, namely the fertilisation of one flower by the pollen from another plant.

He gave many examples from the orchids of the British countryside, but one of his most spectacular was the Madagascar star orchid (*Angraecum sesquipedale*), which has an extremely long nectary (sometimes over 35cm – more than a foot – in length). He argued that this must be an adaptation to attract an insect with an extraordinarily long proboscis. At the time no such creature was known from Madagascar, and the suggestion was ridiculed. However, 20 years after Darwin's death, Karl Jordan and Walter Rothschild discovered, on the great Indian Ocean island, a moth with an appropriately long proboscis (Morgan's sphinx moth), and to which an appropriate scientific name was given: *Xanthopan morgani praedicta*!

As we have seen, from his earliest days on the *Beagle*, Darwin was interested in the behaviour of animals. His interest in two specialized types of plant – climbing plants and insectivorous plants – can be seen as an extension of that work; both can be said to be able to 'perceive' aspects of their environment and to respond to it. Both can be seen as being part of his research on the broad themes of the relationship between organisms and their environment, and that of growth and change.

25. Green-winged orchid (*Orchis morio*). One of the species upon which Darwin experimented to demonstrate the importance of insect pollination. *John and Alison Underwood, North Wales*

Darwin first published an article on climbing plants in the *Journal of the Linnean Society* in 1865; an expanded and corrected form appeared as a monograph in 1875. A second edition appeared in 1882.

Darwin recognized four classes of climbing plants: firstly, twining plants, 'those that twine spirally round a support'; secondly, 'those endowed with irritable organs, which, when they touch any object clasp it', although he accepted that these two classes graduate into one another to some extent. The third class included those that climbed with hooks, and the fourth those that used rootlets.

He then described the manner in which 'leaf climbers' and 'tendril bearers' climb, giving a number of case studies. The extract below, from his account of *Bignonia unguis*, is typical:

> The young shoots revolve ... The stem twines imperfectly around a vertical stick some times reversing its direction ... Each leaf consists of a petiole bearing a pair of leaflets, and terminates in a tendril. ... It is curiously like the leg and foot of a small bird, with the hind toe cut off. The straight leg or tarsus is longer than the three toes, which are of equal length, and diverging, lie in the same plane. The toes terminate in sharp, hard claws, much curved downwards, like those on a bird's foot. ... The whole tendril, namely the tarsus and three toes, are likewise sensitive to contact, especially in their under surfaces. When a shoot grows in the midst of thin branches, the tendrils are soon brought by their revolving movement ... into contact with them; and then one toe of the tendril, or more commonly all three, bend, and after several hours seize fast hold of the twigs, like a bird when perched. If the tarsus of the tendril comes in contact with a twig, it goes on slowly bending, until the whole foot is carried quite round, and the toes pass on each size and seize it. (*Climbing Plants*, Chapter 3)

Here we see evidence of Darwin's careful observation, his attention to detail and his experimental approach. We can also see interesting aspects of his style: he uses simile and metaphor, as he so often did, to get his points across. His description of the movements in plants is very similar to the way in which he might describe a piece of animal behaviour – proof that he saw his work on 'movements and habits' of climbing plants as an extension to his work on animal behaviour, that led to his book on the *Expression of Emotions in Animals and Man* (John Murray, 1872). He emphasizes the theme of adaptation that runs through much of his evolutionary writing.

The book is also a profoundly evolutionary text. He saw twiners, leaf twiners and tendril climbers as members of a series: 'On the view given here leaf-climbers were primordially twiners, and tendril bearers (when formed of modified leaves) were primordially leaf-climbers.' He is also at pains to point out at many places the way in which climbing can be seen as an adaptation to environment: in the tropical forests, climbing allows many species to reach the light of the upper layers of the forest canopy.

In *Insectivorous Plants* he shows how the insectivorous habit (and all that this involves – the secretion of digestive juices by leaves; tentacles that seize a trapped insects) are adaptations that enable a plant to survive in infertile soils.

> The absorption of animal matter from captured insects explains how Drosera can flourish in extremely poor peaty soil, in some cases where nothing but sphagnum moss grows, and mosses depend altogether on the atmosphere for their nourishment. … [C]onsidering the nature of the soil where it grows, the supply of nitrogen would be extremely limited, or quite deficient, unless the plant had the power of obtaining this important element from captured insects. We can thus understand how it is that the roots are so poorly developed. These usually consist of only two or three slightly divided branches, from half to one inch in length, furnished with absorbent hairs. It appears, therefore, that the roots serve only to imbibe water … carbonate of ammonia. A plant of Drosera, with the edges of its leaves curled inwards, so as to form a temporary stomach, with the glands of the closely inflected tentacles pouring forth their acid secretion, which dissolves animal matter, afterwards to be absorbed, may be said to feed like an animal. But, differently from an animal, it drinks by means of its roots … (*Insectivorous Plants*, 1875, Chapter 1)

This is Darwin at his best: it shows careful observation and shrewd deduction, as well as his integrative abilities. It clearly emphasizes the plant's adaptation to environment climate, but also relates the plant's form to its environment and physiology. He is here pushing home the evolutionary message of 'adaptation to environment' that he had stressed 15 years before in the *Origin*.

Darwin's *On the Origin* has often been described as presenting 'one long argument'. The chapters logically follow one on another, and the argument is gradually developed, examples are given and objections met. It can also be said that the whole corpus of his work represents just such a 'long argument'. The evolutionary theme echoes through almost all his books (and many of his papers and articles) from the *Origin* onwards. Themes introduced in one work are developed in others and further examples given. It is as though there was a carefully calculated plan. To some extent there was. For example, in a letter to his publisher about the orchid volume he said: 'I think this little volume will do good to the *Origin*, as it will show that I have worked hard at details.' When one considers the ill health that seems to have plagued Darwin, and the misfortunes that affected him – to the extent that work was often interrupted – the dedication to his task and concentration on the path that he had set himself is truly remarkable.

14

Last Things

For much of his life, although there had been occasional periods of improvement, Charles Darwin did not enjoy good health. It has sometimes been assumed that his illnesses were at least partly psychosomatic, the result of stress caused by appreciation of the effects his revolutionary ideas might have on the world, and of the vigorous, often venomous, criticism he had to withstand following the publication of *On the Origin* and *Descent of Man*.

The pattern of intermittent illness, but a continuing almost compulsive addiction to work, continued into his last years. He was 'Never happy except when at work,' he wrote in his last few months of life. For much of late 1880 and the spring of 1881, although he must have known that he had not very long to live, he worked on his final book, on earthworms. The words came slowly. Perhaps the words of William Shakespeare entered his mind:

Let's talk of graves, of worms and epitaphs. (*King Richard II*, Act 3, Scene 2)

He had enjoyed the bard in his younger years.

Yet the book has a positive, almost optimistic tone – we ought to be grateful to worms, he wrote – and the work is recapitulatory. It includes observations that he had been gathering for years. He had done numerous experiments, and had a 'wormstone' set up in his garden, quite close to the house, with instruments attached to it, to measure the rate of burial of items on the surface of the soil by earthworms.

The final paragraph of this, Darwin's final book, published a matter of months before his death, reads as follows:

It may be doubted whether there are many other animals which have played so important a part in the history of the world, as have these lowly organised creatures. Some other animals, however, still more lowly organised, namely corals have done far more conspicuous work in having reefs and islands in the great oceans; but these are almost confined to the tropical zones. (*Vegetable Mould and Earthworms*, Chapter 7)

Moreover, among the very first scientific papers that Darwin published – both presented to the Geological Society of London, in 1837, very shortly after his return from his voyage – were one on coral reefs, and one on earthworms and 'the formation of mould'. (The coral paper was followed by the first volume of the *Geology of the Voyage of the Beagle* dealing with coral reefs and atolls, published in 1842.) Studies of both earthworms and the tiny coral organisms had occupied him as he started out as a naturalist and at the very end of his scientific career, some 45 years later. On both occasions, and in relation to both groups of organisms, he stressed the great changes that can be wrought by the long-continued action of extremely slow processes. As the theme of gradual change runs though the entire body of Darwin's work, this is of great interest.

Also, this final work (the full title was *The Formation of Vegetable Mould, through the Action of Worms, with Observations on their Habits*) recapitulates a great deal of what Charles Darwin attempted throughout his career. It combines both the 'natural history' or biological approach – the study of organisms – together with the geological approach, the study of the processes that shape the surface of the earth. As the title implies, he considers in detail the behaviour of the earthworms (as we have seen, from the earliest days aboard the *Beagle*, Darwin was ahead of his day in considering the habits and behaviour of animals as well as their morphology). He employed the experimental approach, performing a series of experiments to investigate earthworms' sensitivity to smell, sound, light, vibration and other stimuli, and he also used quantitative methods. He undertook a series of experiments with tree-leaves of different species, and with triangles of paper, to test the worms' ability to recognize them and to manipulate them into the entrances to their burrows. These results were presented in a series of statistical tables.

But perhaps the most important contribution in this book is Darwin's realization of the rate at which objects on the surface of the ground were buried through the regular delivery by worms of castings (pellets or capsules of soil passed out by the earthworms, the organic matter within the soil having been digested and absorbed within their guts) to the surface. As the result of his own many observations and experiments undertaken near his home (including the wormstone experiment), he calculated that there were of the order of 53,880 worms per acre of English farmland.

> If we assume that they work for only half the year – though this is too low an estimate – then the worms in this field would eject during the year 8.387 pounds per square yard; 18.12 tons per acre, assuming the whole surface to be equally productive in castings. (*Vegetable Mould*, Chapter 3)

Darwin backs up these statements by references to the way in which the remnants of ancient buildings – Roman villas and medieval abbeys – have sometimes been almost completely buried by the worms' activities. He also emphasizes the role of worms in creating 'mould', the name he gives to the dark, upper layer of the soil, through their burrowing activities and their pulling down of leaves and other organic material.

A chapter of the book is devoted to 'The action of worms in the denudation of the land'. In this he speculates that the burrowing of worms allows air, water and humic acids to penetrate the soil and to affect the parent rock below. He continues: 'Not only do worms aid indirectly in the chemical disintegration of rocks, but there is good reason to believe that they likewise act in a direct and mechanical manner on the smaller particles.' By breaking up the soil particles that pass through their bodies, they reduce them to a fine powder. The minute particles are thus the more likely to be blown or washed away.

Thus:

> Worms have played a more important part in the history of the world than most persons would at first suppose. In almost all humid countries they are extraordinarily numerous ... In many parts of England a weight of more than ten tons [10,516 kg] of dry earth annually passes through their bodies and is brought to the surface on each acre of land. (*Vegetable Mould*, Chapter 7)

Elsewhere in this, the concluding chapter, he reminds readers that worms have a number of ways of perceiving and reacting to their environment; they are capable of quite complex behaviour in burrowing, in lining their burrows with leaves and, in some species, producing quite elaborate almost tower-like castings. Indeed: 'They act in nearly the manner as would a man, who had to close a cylindrical tube with different kinds of leaves, petioles, triangles of paper, &c., for they commonly seize such objects by their pointed ends.'

In this, the very final chapter of his final book, Darwin therefore sees something of a continuity between lowly creatures and humans; he emphasizes the importance of gradual change in producing enormous effects, and stresses the intimate relationships that exist between organisms and their environment, both biological and physical. These are the three principal themes that run through much of Darwin's life and work.

The work was completed just before Easter 1881. 'I have little strength & feel very old,' he wrote to a friend at the time. He could not embark on another major investigation.

Darwin had had heart palpitations, from time to time, since shortly before the *Beagle* voyage. While visiting London in December 1881 he had serious chest pains. He staggered, stumbled, and grasped onto railings while he was walking along a street. The next day he seemed slightly better, and Dr Clarke, his London physician, declared him well, and he seemed to recover. Back at Down House in early 1882, he worked intermittently on scientific papers, and occasionally walked around the Sandwalk. Nevertheless he was very weak.

A severe cough left him very miserable in February 1882; he vomited frequently and chest pains returned. On 7 March he was again walking slowly around the Sandwalk when he had another seizure; he was alone, but managed to hobble back to the house, collapsing into Emma's arms. Dr Clarke diagnosed angina, and prescribed morphia for the pain, but Charles became depressed, and moved very little for some days. But he improved, and briefly took part in a few family activities. Another doctor, Norman Moore, was reassuring, stating that he just had a weak heart. However, by early April the attacks were becoming more severe. The old naturalist Darwin, although he knew the end was not far off, retained the habits of a scientific lifetime, carefully recording his own symptoms: 'stomach excessively bad' and 'much pain', he recorded, as though his decline was an experiment like those he had conducted years before on his orchids and insectivorous plants. Various medications were prescribed. During a meal on 15 April he felt a violent stabbing pain in the head. He staggered into another room, collapsed onto the sofa, and fell unconscious. 'Dropped down,' he later noted. It is recorded that he said to Emma, 'It's almost worthwhile to be sick to be nursed by you.' Although there were lucid times, the next couple of days he was racked by pain, was nauseous and frequently fell unconscious. He died in the afternoon of Wednesday 19 April 1882, in Emma's arms, just a little over two months after his seventy-third birthday. Not long before he passed he was heard to utter, 'I am not at least afraid to die.' He appreciated that his work was done, and that there was completeness to his life.

The family hoped for Charles to be buried quietly in the churchyard at Downe, close to the graves of his brother Erasmus and two of his dead infant children; the village carpenter prepared a coffin. But John Lubbock, long-time neighbour, friend and disciple, intervened. John was a prosperous banker and an influential member of Parliament, and he persuaded some 20 co-Parliamentarians to petition the Dean of Westminster, suggesting to him 'that it would be acceptable to a very large number of our fellow countrymen … that our illustrious countryman, Dr Darwin, should be buried in Westminster Abbey'. The press mounted a campaign, journalists seeing such an event as an important gesture of 'reconciliation between Faith and Science'. His great friend and erstwhile 'bulldog', Thomas Huxley, also put pressure on the Abbey clergy. Reluctantly, Emma and the family agreed: they thought he would have 'wished to accept' the nation's 'acknowledgement of what he had done'.

Darwin's pallbearers at the funeral, which was held at noon on 26 April 1882, were: Joseph Hooker, his great friend and botanist colleague; his 'bulldog', zoologist Thomas Huxley; Alfred Russel Wallace, co-originator of the theory of evolution through natural selection; and his friend, supporter and neighbour John Lubbock. Behind followed dignitaries of church and state:

his eldest son William was chief mourner; the rest of the family, representatives of scientific bodies, the universities, and from the USA, Russia and many countries of Europe also accompanied the coffin. One commentator referred to 'the greatest gathering of intellect … ever brought together'.

As the procession made its way through the Abbey, a specially written anthem was sung: the words were from the Old Testament book of Proverbs: 'Happy is the man that findeth wisdom and getteth understanding.'

Darwin, agnostic though he was, was buried in the Abbey in what has become known as 'scientists' corner'. He was laid beneath the monument to physicist Sir Isaac Newton, quite close to his friend the geologist Charles Lyell, and to his mentor, the astronomer Sir John Herschel, whose book on scientific method he had read as an undergraduate, encouraging him to make a contribution to science himself, and whom he had met in Cape Town towards the end of the *Beagle*'s voyage.

Although certain voices were raised, before and after the funeral, against the pomp associated with it, by those who felt that the great naturalist's ideas were an evil blasphemy, on the whole the dignity attached to the proceedings was felt by the British nation and the world to have been appropriate for a distinguished Englishman, the greatest of all naturalists.

15

Good luck or bad luck?

Taking Charles Darwin's life as a whole it would be difficult to come to any other conclusion than that good fortune predominated over bad. Scientifically he had enormous success: for example he was elected to the Royal Society just before he was 30, and later received the Copley and Royal Medals from that organization. Although some of Cambridge's clerical academics opposed Darwin's evolutionary ideas vehemently, within his lifetime his ideas came largely to be accepted by the scientific community, to the extent that in November 1877, 18 years after the publication of the first edition of *On the Origin of Species*, he returned in triumph to his alma mater, to receive an honorary degree. The occasion was a highly spectacular one with his wife Emma and some of his children in the audience. Undergraduates filled the galleries, stood in the windows, and perched on statues, shouting and laughing. A puppet monkey frolicked above the crowd on a cord strung across the hall in which the ceremony was to be performed. Later the 'missing link', a ring decorated with bright ribbons, appeared. Students cheered. After a speech in Latin was given describing the great naturalist's achievements, Darwin beamed at the crowds.

In the latter part of his life he was a wealthy man. Part of his fortune was inherited, but he was reasonably economical, and made some shrewd investments (although some were less than completely successful).

He had the affection of a number of extremely influential friends, who at certain critical times went out of their way to support him. He had a network of some 2,000 correspondents in many countries who willingly supplied him with information, specimens or helped in other ways. He came from a large family and married into another. His extended family assisted him in a multitude of ways, sometimes only at the mundane level of providing a week's accommodation when ill health and overwork got him down. His wife and family adored him, and some went on to achieve spectacular success in their own right. He lived long enough to see his son George elected to the Royal Society; two others followed, along with a grandson.

His lost his mother at a young age, and his father was in some respects a difficult man. But the love of his sisters, his cousins and the stalwart support of his uncle (and later father-in-law), Josiah Wedgwood, to some extent made up for this. When Dr Robert Darwin opposed his son's embarking on the *Beagle* voyage as 'a waste of time', Josiah firmly but gently pointed out the advantages.

Good fortune indeed.

It was perhaps chance that Darwin visited so many different environments, and visited them in a particular order (see Chapter 7). The appearance of *Archaeopteryx* within a few years of the publication of *On the Origin* was completely unexpected. But Darwin had the knack of 'making his own luck'. He generally replied to his correspondents promptly. He reciprocated the kindnesses received from friends and relations. He had the knack of getting on well with people of all sorts, races and social classes. Although not a conscious 'networker', he developed friendships and personal links from his Cambridge days (and even to some extent before, while at Edinburgh) that he was able to utilize profitably later. Not studying much science at Cambridge, nevertheless the links with Henslow and Sedgwick provided, both in the fields of East Anglia and in North Wales, just enough training. It was through the Cambridge network that the *Beagle* offer came. Friendships made on the *Beagle* were then utilized in the search for information, obtaining specimens, and to some extent in getting material published.

He was dogged by ill health for much of the latter part of his life – possibly he was affected by the rigours of the voyage, possibly he suffered from psychosomatic symptoms, conceivably some of his indisposition was inherited. Sometimes he was unable to work for weeks at a time; sometimes he was only able to do an hour or two a day. Three of his children died. But Emma nursed him, loved him and supported him through thick and thin. And despite his ailments, his pace of work was relentless. For much of his life he continuously had the manuscript of a major book 'on the go'. Sometimes several. Not to mention the stream of scientific papers that he churned out. Many were brilliant. A very few were flops: such was his paper on the Parallel Roads of Glen Roy, beach-like features high on a Scottish hillside, which, like benches he saw on the coast of South America and elsewhere, he thought were cut when the sea was at a higher level than now. It turned out the 'roads' were cut by an ice-dammed lake at the end of the Ice Age, and he had to acknowledge that the paper was a 'great failure'.

But things might have been very different. If he had not been determined enough to go against Dr Robert Darwin's wishes and leave Edinburgh unqualified, he might have, reluctantly, become a small-town doctor like his father and grandfather. If he had chanced to meet his ex-girlfriend Fanny Owen in Plymouth on the eve of the ship's sailing he might have married her and retired to a country rectory. She would have been bored, and she would probably not have nursed him as lovingly as Emma.

If that 'third wave' had overwhelmed the *Beagle* south of Cape Horn all would have perished. If the organism that bit him in South America had infected him (or infected him more seriously than it did) he would have perished, either on the voyage or some years thereafter. He might have drowned, as did one of his shipmates, searching for specimens amidst the tangled kelp beds of East Falkland or Tierra del Fuego. Some of the fish he ate seem to have been poisonous, yet he survived. He wandered out on coral reefs, in Tahiti, and probably also at Cocos; he might have fallen, been dragged across the rocks by a wave. In South America he experienced an earthquake and saw the devastating results of a tsunami. The ship might have been wrecked on the coast of Australia. The splash-wave from crashing into the channel of ice from the glacier in Tierra del Fuego might, but for his own quick thinking, have overwhelmed the small boat in which the group was exploring, leaving him and his companions isolated among hostile Fuegans with little food or equipment. He might have had an accident in the high

Andes. He might have been thrown from his horse and broken his back, as he galloped over the pampas, been killed by brigands, or got in the way of the firefight in Montevideo.

So, like many, he was dealt a mixed hand. Personal tragedy and debilitating handicaps were intermixed with amazing good fortune. While travelling, the necessary risks taken to secure the specimens he sought and the observations he was determined to make were balanced by a certain caution. His natural attributes of courtesy, easy politeness and tolerance meant that many were able and willing to help him, even where they were different from him in background, social class or on certain matters of belief.

There are analogies between Darwin's life and work and the theory for which he is best known – the evolution of life on earth as the result of natural selection. Moreover, recent developments in science have allowed the elaboration and confirmation of Darwin's original concepts. There is a randomness about life, but there is also something of a structure, a directionality.

Natural selection is dependent on variation in populations of organisms; some variations are within a normal range (in height in humans, in the intensity of colour in a flower's petals), but some variations are unpredictable. Today we understand that mutations occur in every generation – as the result of radiation, chemicals in the environment or when 'errors' appear as the DNA is copied. Changes in the DNA are linked to changes in the character of the organism.

The appearance of these changes appears to be random – simply a matter of chance.

What is more predictable is that unfavourable characteristics will tend to be eliminated by natural selection. Possibly the selection occurs actually at the level of the embryo, so that the organism never develops; possibly later, reducing the chance – the probability – that the characteristic will be passed to the next generation. 'Favourable' characters increase the chance of survival, and the likelihood that the character, and the gene on which it is based, is handed on to the next generation, and the generation after that … and so on.

Darwin did not understand the nature of genetics: 'The laws governing inheritance are quite unknown,' he wrote at an early point in *On the Origin*. Although Darwin was an approximate contemporary of the abbot Gregor Mendel (1822–84) of Brünn (now Brno), the monk's ideas were not publicized until much later. And of course molecular biology and the unravelling of the DNA helix lay far in the future. But he did understand the chanciness of variation, and the notion that the higher a population the higher the probability of a beneficial variation appearing. In Chapter 1 of *On the Origin*, that on 'Variation under domestication', we see:

> But as variations manifestly useful or pleasing to man appear only occasionally, the chance of their appearance will be much increased by a large number of individuals being kept; and hence this comes to be of the highest importance to success. On this principle Marshall has remarked, with respect to the sheep in parts of Yorkshire, that 'as they generally belong to poor people, and are mostly *in small lots*, they can never be improved'. On the other hand nurserymen, from raising large stocks of the same plants, are generally far more successful in getting new and valuable varieties. (Italics in original)

And in the book that extended his work on domestication of animals and plants:

> Lord Rivers, when asked how he succeeded in always having first-rate greyhounds, answered, 'I breed many, and hang many.' This, as another man remarks, 'was the secret of his success; and the same will be found in exhibiting fowls, – successful competitors breed largely, and keep the best.' (*Animals and Plants under Domestication*, Volume 2, Chapter 21)

Darwin in his work clearly understood the importance of chance and the evolutionary significance of rare occurrences.

Darwin made important discoveries based on the various remote islands he visited. His sojourn in the Galapagos, and the specimens he collected there, are best known, but he also noted endemic creatures in the Falklands, Ascension Island and elsewhere.

This is ironic, as endemism, or uniqueness, is particularly common on remote islands. Part of the reason for this is the process now described as the process of 'genetic drift'. Variations or mutations that have little effect on sur-viviorship – those that are 'neutral' – may be swamped in a large population. But in a very small, isolated population, this may not happen, and a random variation, neither beneficial nor harmful to its possessor, may survive in the population by pure chance. A dramatic collapse of the population may have the same effect. If a population of organisms is reduced by disease, by some catastrophe such as a volcanic upheaval, or a typhoon, or even overhunting by humans, it may be pure chance whether particular individuals, and the genes they contain, will survive or be eliminated. Whether the combination of characters that the few survivors possess is beneficial or not, they will dominate the populations of succeeding generations. This could be called the 'survival of the luckiest not the fittest' (*New Scientist*, No. 2652, 18 April 2008, 'Evolution: a guide for the not yet perplexed'). It has been argued that if some different combination of the strange organisms that existed in the remote Cambrian period of the earth's history had 'been lucky' and survived, the whole of the history of life might have been different.

Thus in the life of the originator of the concept of evolution, so with evolution itself, chance plays an important role.

But just as there was a directionality in Darwin's scientific work, so there was in the evolution of life on earth. From the first glimmerings of the notion of gradualism, as developed in his theory of coral reefs, through the stumblings and gropings in his early notebooks, to the 'Sketch', to the 'Essay' and his book *On the Origin of Species* itself. Then on through *Animals and Plants under Domestication, Descent of Man, Emotions* and the series of botanical volumes to the recapitulatory *Earthworm* volume, the same set of ideas can be traced. As with the branching tree of life that Darwin envisaged, these concepts branch and subdivide, sometimes taking on a life of their own. But (although exceptions exist) there is a trend from simple to complex. From the 'primaeval slime', or at least the very simplest organisms of the Pre-Cambrian, to modern humanity. Within each phylum, or evolutionary direction, development can be traced. Occasionally intermediates or transitional forms between the major groups have been found. *Archaeopteryx* has an intermediate place between the reptiles and birds (see page 163).

Even more sensational is *Tiktaalik*, a fossil organism apparently intermediate between fish and land animals found in Devonian rocks in the Canadian Arctic, the discovery of which was published early in 2006. Several examples of a creature called *Tiktaalik roseae* (the name *Tiktaalik* means, in the Inuit language Inuktikuk, 'large shallow-water fish') were found in deposits laid down in a tropical river delta about 354 to 417 million years ago in Ellesmere Island. The animal was about 2.75 metres (9 feet) long and probably resembled a crocodile. The creature had bony scales and fins, but the front fins have the internal skeleton structure of an arm, with wrists and elbows, but fins instead of separate fingers. The lower jaw and palate are also similar to those in primitive fish (sarcopterygians). The animal had a structure on its head that resembles a gill-slit, described as 'on its way to becoming an ear', and an elongated snout that would have helped it to catch prey when on land.

Some might see the directionality of organic evolution as similar to that of Darwin's life and work. Be that as it may, it is reasonable to say that his life mixture of good and ill fortune, that was directional in some regards, but not in all, to some extent influenced by his own determination and character but to some extent influenced by random events, is a mirror for the life of Everyman as well as an allegory for the tangled miracle of life itself.

Index